The Evolving Virtual Library II

Practical and Philosophical Perspectives

The Evolving Virtual Library II

Practical and Philosophical Perspectives

Edited by Laverna M. Saunders

Information Today, Inc.

Medford, NJ

Copyright © 1999 by Information Today, Inc.
143 Old Marlton Pike
Medford, NJ 08055

Printed in the United States of America

The Library of Congress has cataloged the preceding volume as follows:

The evolving virtual library II: practical and philosophical perspectives edited by
  Laverna Saunders.
    p. cm.
    Volume developed from a session of the Eighth Annual Computers in Libraries
Conference.
    Includes bibliographical references and index.
    ISBN 1-57387-070-6 (hardcover: alk. paper)
    1. Libraries—United States—Automation—Congresses. 2. Online
information services—United States—Congresses. 3. Library
information networks—United States—Congresses. 4. Digital
libraries—United States—Congresses. I. Saunders, Laverna, M.
II. Computers in Libraries Conference (8th : 1993 : Washington,
D.C.)
Z678.A4U633   1995
025′.00285—dc20

                                       95-39544
                                       CIP

Price: $39.50

Publisher: Thomas H. Hogan, Sr.
Editor-in-Chief: John B. Bryans
Managing Editor: Janet M. Spavlik
Production Manager: M. Heide Dengler
Cover Design: Adam Vinick
Book Design: Patricia F. Kirkbride
Indexer: Laurie Andriot

Contents

Preface

A decade has passed since the term "virtual library" first entered our professional vocabulary. During this period the Internet has become an essential part of library network infrastructure and services, and the Web now provides links to essential electronic resources located on-site and off-site. The dedicated dumb terminal that displayed the online catalog of the local system has been replaced by a PC or Macintosh that serves as a gateway to a growing body of bibliographic and full-text information. The catalog is now represented by a desktop icon or a menu item on a home page, surrounded by many other listings or icons that are linked through the infrastructure of the Web.

The content of libraries is also changing, most notably in serial publications. Tables of print indexes have given way to online databases that may include full-text articles or abstracts as well as citations for articles. Through individual or consortium contracts with vendors, libraries may offer more journals electronically than they subscribe to in print form. Newspapers and reference resources that are time sensitive can be updated electronically and are available on the Web for access at anytime, now referred to as "7 x 24". Web access to digital content has created a ripple effect for library functions and jobs at the same time that it has extended the library on a global scale.

The chapters included in this volume address many of the practical and philosophical issues encountered in the process of developing the virtual library. A number of research libraries have developed innovative projects using grant funding and/or local computing resources. Public, special, and K-12 libraries are also developing local databases and Web sites which provide useful content to their user communities.

The first chapter introduces the concept of the virtual library and explores how the increasing reliance on computers and digital information has affected users and staff. In particular, technology has produced an expectation for full-text information delivered to the desktop at the user's convenience. As the technologies used by libraries have evolved, library jobs, organizational structures, and working conditions have changed. Some facets of the virtual library present challenges to the intellectual, social, and physical needs of adults and children. In the midst of technological change, the traditional library mission of service and access is still relevant, and librarians are needed more than ever before to teach new information literacy skills and to help users cope with changing technologies.

Judith Field begins with a historical view of library automation, especially within the context of corporate and other special libraries. In the last decade research organizations and business corporations have implemented specialized telecommunications networks called Intranets and Extranets. Field describes the functions of these types of networks, and their implications for special libraries. Working with networks requires that librarians acquire additional professional competencies in order to promote and ensure the value of the library to the organization. One primary opportunity for special librarians is managing the content of the corporation's knowledge management system. By creating and maintaining customized links to Web resources, librarians can serve all staff and selected customers, wherever they may be. Librarians can also use push technology to provide critical and timely information to users. Intranets and Extranets give librarians new opportunities to collaborate with MIS departments and clients in designing useful information systems.

One of the primary values of networks is supporting access to digital content. The Making of America (MoA) project at the University of Michigan is an important initiative aimed at preserving and making available primary sources for nineteenth century United States history. A further purpose of MoA is developing protocols for the selection, conversion, storage, retrieval, and use of digitized information on a large-scale, distributed basis. As one of the principals working on the project, Maria Bonn describes the scope of the venture and its evolutionary path. She also shares how librarians were instrumental in developing system and intellectual architectures to make MoA workable and easy for novices to use. By distributing MoA through the Web, the University of Michigan has placed this valuable resource on the desktop of users all over the globe.

The Scholarly Communications Project (SCP) at Virginia Tech provides another model for creating and integrating digital resources within the services offered by a research library. Gail McMillan, director of SCP, reviews a number of innovative projects initiated during the past decade. The formats converted and serviced by Virginia Tech include reserves, dissertations and theses, journals, news reports, international newspapers, archival images, and instructional slides. This case study also illustrates the productivity and resourcefulness of a dedicated, small unit operating within an institution that is committed to using technology to enhance instruction and research.

Nearly every library has an information access problem that could be solved by the creation of a local database. Librarians at the University Library of Tromsø used off-the-shelf database and customized tools to create Internet-accessible files that promote physical library resources such as new books and recently received journals. As Tore Brattli explains in his chapter, such locally created databases offer the advantages of control over information, search options, and presentation format. They are useful as customized reference resources and as collection management and statistical tools. Finally, local databases can be linked to other electronic documents and files through the library's Web site, providing global access.

The market on Web-accessible databases is not limited to university libraries by any means. The St. Joseph County Public Library (SJCPL) in South Bend, Indiana, was an early adopter of Internet and database technologies at each step of the evolutionary path. Director Don Napoli recounts the transitions that his organization made as it became the first public library in the United States to run its own Web server and home page. The global aspects of the virtual library became apparent to SJCPL when the City Library of Helsinki, Finland, the first public library on the Web, shared information and invited Napoli to speak at a conference. In addition to having a Web-accessible OPAC, SJCPL also provides locally generated databases of community information. Staff and user training is a priority for SJCPL, and librarians offer free Internet classes to the public each month.

The teaching function is likewise a primary mission for school libraries. High school librarian Joyce Kasman Valenza outlines how educational reform and the constructivist approach to learning require school libraries to be true learning environments. Librarians are needed more than ever to prepare students for productive use of vast information resources. In addition, a variety of formats should be available on-site for student investigation and multimedia production. Valenza also highlights model home pages that school librarians have created as effective teaching tools, links to classroom work, and support for independent research by students.

The growing trend for distance learning has raised issues about appropriate library services. Vicky York, Distance Education Coordinator at Montana

State University Libraries, asserts that library services are integral to distance learning. The challenges facing libraries include funding additional electronic services and publications and providing equal access for remote students. Research indicates that academic libraries are offering online catalog access, e-mail and phone reference, home delivery of books and articles, resources at satellite centers, electronic reserves, and bibliographic instruction. New guidelines are now available to help libraries plan for distance learning, and librarians need to collaborate with distance learning providers. Our traditional methods of teaching, learning, and research have not changed as fast as the technologies for distributing information. Librarians have an important role to play in teaching learners to evaluate electronic sources and in helping students succeed wherever they are located.

The virtual library is supported by a combination of local and global telecommunications and network infrastructure. Providing a general overview and survival primer, George Machovec defines the technical terms, identifies the basic elements, and reviews the functions of network typologies currently used by libraries. Infrastructure and bandwidth determine the library's ability to deliver digital content and will be increasingly critical to the evolving virtual library. Plans for service and digital information must include the costs of upgrading terminals and adding hardware and software to support network capacity. If the library staff is not responsible for maintaining the network, then collaboration with information technology or computer center staff is critical for troubleshooting, training, and planning. Network structure and security also determine who has access to what, and authentication for distant learners or remote users must be considered as design and administration elements. Machovec also covers the critical issues that librarians need to consider in planning functional networks as telecommunications technologies and international policies and standards continue to change.

Marshall Keys, executive director of NELINET, closes the volume with an assessment of where libraries are headed. We have lived with the evolutionary changes of the past twenty years and can expect revolutionary changes in the next twenty years. Keys sees the library continuing as a physical place with staff and hybrid collections. The notable differences will include growing external control of digital collections and the standards by which they are accessed. More of the traditional library functions of decision making and cataloging will be automated or outsourced, and librarians will need new managerial skills such as negotiating. The new information economy, which includes scholarly publishing, information aggregators, metadata, technology, and consortia, will create stress but will vastly improve information resources for users.

The librarians invited to contribute chapters for this book have extensive experience in their respective areas of expertise. My objectives in compiling this volume include documenting trends which are making libraries more virtual, providing timely information about current issues, and presenting challenging concerns which will require thought and experimentation to resolve. Many forces are driving the changes in our internal and external environments, and awareness is the first step to influencing the future.

Laverna M. Saunders, editor
June 1999

The Virtual Library:
Reflections on an Evolutionary Process

Laverna M. Saunders, Ed.D.
Dean of the Library, Instructional & Learning Support
Salem State College
Salem, Massachusetts

INTRODUCTION

As library staff has become accustomed to working with computers and digital content, it is hard to imagine a library without them. In my first paraprofessional job in a technical services department twenty-five years ago, we used various Library of Congress book catalogs as the source of our cataloging. I was thrilled when the Mansell Pre-1956 volumes were published, and I was nearly ecstatic when we received a Kellogg grant to become an OCLC member. Since that time, there has been no looking back—except perhaps once a few years ago when I had to retire the Mansell set and its oak bookcases to other parts of the building in order to make room for workstations hosting networked electronic resources.

The current generation of college students has never known a world without PCs. Most young children live in homes that contain a wide variety of digital devices, and they are challenged to tell time with an analog clock. A growing number of families own a computer and subscribe to a commercial Internet service. When these users come to the library, they expect to find networked computers as well as other resources.

Technological change continues to be a dominant force reshaping society and culture, and especially libraries. The virtual library is an evolutionary phenomenon that increasingly incorporates digital technologies and content, as a complement to traditional print resources, to meet user need. As technology has changed our lives, it has increased user expectations for the library. Likewise, it has redefined library jobs, the organizational structure, and working conditions. While benefiting from the increased information and access of the virtual library, we also need to be aware of technology's negative elements. Ultimately we need to affirm our traditional values as we continue the process of change.

DEFINING THE VIRTUAL LIBRARY

During the decade of the 1990s the term "virtual library" became a recognized phrase for describing libraries that offer access to digital information by using a variety of networks, including the Internet and World Wide Web. Other synonyms used interchangeably with virtual library are "library without walls" and "electronic" or "digital" library. The virtual library includes digital content that can be delivered anytime and anywhere to a networked computer. Gapen presents a holistic sense of the virtual library as "remote access to the contents and services of libraries and other information resources, combining an on-site collection of current and heavily used materials in both print and electronic form, with an electronic network which provides access to, and delivery from, external worldwide library and commercial information and knowledge sources" (1993, p. 1). Essentially, the virtual library is a metaphor for the networked library (von Wahlde, 1993).

USERS' EXPECTATIONS

Digital technology has changed our concept of time. Because computers retrieve and process information rapidly, users expect speed in all aspects of their lives, including their transactions with the library. "The modern user knows it is possible to use an automatic teller card across the country to obtain cash; to change airline and hotel reservations from a car phone; and to fax a copy of an article to Australia. Is it any wonder that our users get frustrated when they can't get what they want when they want it?" (Metz, 1990, p. 31).

This transition has occurred over the last fifteen years with the evolution of library technology running in tandem with technological change generally. The online catalog gave users flexibility in using keywords and combining terms. When the online system went down, users waited for it to come back up instead of going to a backup card or microfiche format. Then when users discovered the speed and ease-of-use of searching bibliographic databases on CD-ROM, they used print indexes reluctantly and only when an electronic version did not exist. Such behavior patterns have continued and expanded, to the point where users expect full-text content delivered over the Internet to a workstation in their home or office. As libraries increase the menu of electronic resources, users demand even more. In reflecting on society's expectation for instant gratification, Tenopir states, "the TV/Nintendo/fast food generation expects more and wants it faster. A two-week lag time for interlibrary loan doesn't cut it anymore" (1997, p. 39).

On the positive side, the Internet functions as the primary infrastructure for the virtual library and enables searchers to access resources such as electronic papers, news groups, and e-mail discussions that were not available in the past. To a great extent, the Internet has changed the way students and scholars now do research. According to Doran, "pre-computerized, pre-networked searching restricted people to a largely linear approach, whereby topics and sources had to be examined sequentially in fixed formats and locations. But the Internet is omnidirectional, geographically and chronologically. Separate categories of sources and differences in format are merging" (1996, p. 8). Now users can locate unique historical items that have been digitized, integrate multimedia elements, and import electronic full-text files into new documents for word processing.

The popularity of the Internet has also spawned the misperception that any information that one might want is available free, without having to visit a physical library. While a vast amount of information is indeed accessible through the Web, one must have the necessary equipment, an Internet account, basic searching skills, an extensive period of time, and the ability to evaluate the quality of search results. I suspect that individuals who are satisfied with the hit-and-run approach to research are not even aware of what they are missing. From a professional perspective, the Internet affirms how the theory and practice of traditional librarianship are still relevant. Left to their own devices, students would not "think to use a print index in tandem with an online database" (Doran, 1996, p. 10). Librarians have an enormous challenge in educating students and faculty about good, bad, and even ugly Web content. More than ever before, partnerships with teachers are critical for designing appropriate assignments that require multiple formats and critical thinking.

ENHANCED JOB SKILLS

At the end of the 1990s, all of the staff in libraries use computers and digital content to perform their work. A desirable employee is adept with the functions of word processing programs, can design and manipulate spreadsheets, may know how to create a database, is familiar with the Internet and is willing to use e-mail regularly, and can switch from one system to another and remember the searching protocols for each. The best employees experiment to find new ways to use the capacity of their networked workstation to solve work problems and to try to improve efficiency and effectiveness; they are not afraid to do basic troubleshooting when something does not work. Managers are thrilled to find staff, professional or paraprofessional, who have these attributes. Frequent training opportunities are necessary for staff at all levels, however, because technology changes constantly.

Professional librarians are similarly challenged to stay current with the technology and with strategies to manage change and supervise staff who may have greater technological skills. Woodsworth (1998) discovered that employers look for recent library school graduates who can display their home pages on the Web, have traditional information management competencies but who can use them in high-end technological environments, and who can manage information to improve decision making across the organization. A recent position announcement for an academic librarian included such required qualifications as experience with a networked computing environment, development of electronic delivery of services, Web searching and Web page development, knowledge of HTML, development and delivery of technology-oriented instruction, experience in reference services, and knowledge of information sources in a variety of formats. Both new and long-term professionals need the information skills of the past plus mastery of new technology and its applications.

Library schools now provide continuing education programs geared at helping seasoned librarians improve their knowledge of information technology. The Palmer School of Library and Information Science, for example, helps librarians develop competencies in Internet applications, search engines, evaluation of searches, digital library services, and electronic resources. It also has developed a new program on leading and managing change which involves concepts such as training trainers, working collaboratively with outside agencies, and treating users as customers (Woodsworth, 1998). The concept of lifelong learning has become popular, and librarians across the organization need the opportunities and support to stay current.

Professional listservs provide another avenue for staff at all levels to stay current with changes in their area of responsibility and to network with peers around the world. Paraprofessional staff, for example, can benefit from the ideas shared on LibSup-L, a listserv based at the University of Washington and dedicated to their concerns. Listservs are invaluable for the posting of questions and receipt of quick answers. Listservs and e-mail continue to facilitate decision making and communication, and they help librarians in single-person operations or remote areas feel connected to the profession.

TRANSFORMED ORGANIZATIONS

As libraries and their parent organizations have wired buildings, campuses, schools, and corporations for network access, organizations and jobs have changed. Ready access to information and people presents a challenge to hierarchies and reporting structures. In theory, the network connections of the virtual library have the potential to transform the work environment as staff at all levels communicate more effectively and participate in decision-making processes. The reality is that transformation occurs only when everyone in the organization has the requisite equipment and connectivity and willingly contributes to the process. Virtual meetings do not work if any members neglect to check their e-mail on a regular basis.

Following the trend in business, some libraries have created functional work teams and others have eliminated the traditional hierarchy and moved to flat organizations. What model works best depends on the culture of the institution and the willingness of individuals to support the structure that is established. Despite the availability of technology, effectiveness within the organization is still dependent upon human factors such as leadership, collegiality, cooperation, and a service philosophy that everyone adopts and adheres to.

Technology has also created new jobs and eliminated other ones. Positions such as Webmaster, Electronic Resources Librarian, Distance

Learning Librarian, and Information Literacy Librarian did not exist prior to the integration of the Web into library services. With the growing need to assist users in how to use the computer system and to find electronic content, the public services area has expanded. Concurrently, some libraries have reduced their technical services staff by outsourcing specific acquisitions and cataloging tasks to book jobbers who subcontract with service bureaus. Another form of job redesign is the formation of partnerships between staff in Information Technology, Instructional Media, and faculty. This "dream team" approach has been effective in producing online teaching modules for students to access on campus and from remote locations (see http://www.ohiolink.net/).

TECHNOSTRESS

All of the changes in organizations, job definitions, and required skills have produced anxiety and tension for library staff. The virtual library has evolved over a period of years, and staff who have worked through wiring projects, network development, and numerous upgrades carry emotional baggage which is sometimes revealed in cynicism and negativity.

In 1984, Craig Brod identified a condition called technostress as "a modern disease of adaptation caused by an inability to cope with the new computer technology in a healthy manner" (p. 16). Extrapolating from Brod's work, school librarian Sandra Champion (1988) identified a number of technostress symptoms within the library environment: anxiety, denial, resistance, technophobia, panic, conflict, mental fatigue, intolerance, perfectionism, and physical discomfort. These symptoms are indicators of such fears as losing autonomy, promotional opportunities, control over work environment and freedom and privacy; being isolated and unable to keep up with rapid change; and feeling intimidated by documentation.

Writing more than twenty years after Brod, psychologist Weil and educator Rosen describe the more subtle impact of technology on our lives in terms of irritation from pagers and cellular phones, the feeling that we should be able to work as fast as our computers, the sense that we never have enough time, and the feeling of being behind because we do not know how to surf the Web as well as our children (1997, p. viii). Countering Brod's definition of technostress as a disease, Weil and Rosen define it "as any negative impact on attitudes, thoughts, behaviors, or body physiology that is caused either directly or indirectly by technology" (p. 5).

Keys predicts that the technostress experienced by library staff will soon be felt by users in the form of "info rage" (1998, p. 7). He states that the positive aspects of technology allow librarians to achieve things never dreamed of a few years ago. Now our users have come to expect more of libraries and will possibly turn to anger and violence if denied what they want. More than ever, librarians need to help users understand the difference between what they want and what they need online.

One information technologist, E. Willner, echoes this same phenomenon, "we are now synchronized to Internet time, expected to change our data representations and our tool sets as frequently as we change our clothes" (1998, p. 54). He asserts that frequent changes in moving from one word processing format to another and one typesetting format to another actually have a negative impact on productivity and produce a loss of information in the translation.

Most institutions strive for a computer on every desktop and a three-year replacement cycle. Even in this best-case scenario, standards are decided by a technology department, and library staff have little control over what technology they use, inadequate training on how to use it, and little respite from the constant stream of information and innovation. The top five complaints of employees surveyed by Weil and Rosen (1997) are system problems, computer errors, the time it takes to learn new technology, the reality that time-saving technology seems to end up requiring more work rather than less work, and the fact that technology is always changing too fast to keep up.

ERGONOMICS

Working in the virtual library, staff and users often sit in front of computers for extended periods of time. Beginning with the days when libraries converted card catalogs to online format, staff have become more aware of physical problems resulting from intense computer use. Eye strain, neck pain, and repetitive strain injuries such as carpal tunnel syndrome have affected numerous computer users. Ergonomics is generally accepted as the term for the field of study that considers human performance and well-being in relation to the job, the equipment, and the environment. As applied to the library environment, ergonomics includes the safety and health of both staff and users, their comfort, and their productivity and efficiency.

As libraries have expanded the installation of computers, they have had to invest in workstation furniture that allows the proper placement of computer monitor, keyboard, mouse, and document holders. Chairs used for computer work should have adjustable height and back support and should be on wheels for ease of movement. Accessories may include antiglare screens that fit over the computer display glass and foot rests that reduce stress. In libraries where staff share a common workstation (OCLC terminals, for example), adjustable chairs are a necessity. These chairs will also wear out faster because they are used by multiple individuals. Allowing staff to customize their individual workspace to fit their physical needs supports their willingness to adapt to changing technology and improves their productivity.

Too often the public computer areas are upgraded last. Lacking funds for replacement, libraries usually recycle reading room tables as computer workstations. Inevitably these tables are too high, and their matching oak chairs are too low. These furnishings do not encourage users to do research for long periods of time. As libraries have the opportunity to construct electronic classrooms, they must factor in the cost of appropriate furniture. Likewise, as K-12 libraries incorporate computers, they need to identify furniture that allows children of different ages to be comfortable (Clyde, 1994).

A secondary consideration in the arrangement of computers is the need for variety and privacy. Selected workstations may be arranged for express service with stand-up-only access. Work areas with a place for books and papers may be needed in computer labs. The distance to networked printers and the ease of using debit-card printers should be factored into the arrangement of furniture. Librarians who supervise labs and electronic resource areas need to be able to see users who require assistance. Finally, some users will want privacy to view content which others may consider offensive. Anticipating the needs of individual users and organizing public computer areas accordingly minimize complaints and problems.

ISSUES REGARDING CHILDREN

While research and academic libraries supporting scholars have contributed substantially to the infrastructure and content of the virtual library, the extent of the benefits has been much broader. Children in schools and public libraries are now able to search databases and electronic encyclopedias, communicate with e-mail, compare notes with others in chat rooms, and play games with network users anywhere on the planet. Pen pals have evolved into key pals as children around the globe communicate with each other, develop an awareness of life in other countries and cultures, and affirm their similarities.

In an effort to extend the Internet and its potential for helping children learn, many communities and school districts are involved in projects to wire schools and libraries. An amendment to the Telecommunications Act of 1996 authorized subsidies for Internet connectivity for libraries and schools. Although libraries anticipated benefits such as discounted rates, the telecommunications companies have stalled implementation. Progress continues as funding becomes available, but the disparities between affluent and poor communities and between ethnic and socioeconomic groups are factors that affect children's access to Internet resources.

Concern about the appropriateness of Internet content for children has created conflicts in many communities. Many adults do not want children to have access to those Internet sites that contain sexually explicit or other offensive content. In 1996, Congress passed the Communications Decency Act, which mandated fines and jail sentences for Internet content providers who distributed indecent materials to minors. Then, in 1997, the United States Supreme Court ruled that the act was unconstitutional because it was too broad and lacked the precision that the First Amendment requires when a statute regulates the content of speech. In some cities, including Boston, Austin, and Seattle, the city government has decreed that public libraries must install filtering software to block objectionable sites from children (Schuyler, 1997). The American Library Association has actively protested against filters as constituting censorship. Preferring a proactive approach, ALA offers advice to families on responsible use of the Internet by children (http://www.ala.org). The controversy over filters and First Amendment rights continues to be an issue for schools and public libraries and parallels the longstanding issues that libraries have confronted on the censorship of print materials. Families who allow children unsupervised use of the Internet also have decisions to make about the issue. The Internet brings into the home or library images that would not have been purchased or promoted in a print format.

The pressure for children to use computers has even filtered down to the preschool population, and families are purchasing computers for children who cannot even read. Researchers in early child development claim that the pendulum has swung too far. They are finding that children can be damaged psychologically and physically by spending too much time alone at a computer when they should be playing outdoors and participating in activities with other children and family (Healey, 1998).

RECOGNIZING THE DARK SIDE

Other social problems such as hate mail, stalking, and harassment have migrated to the Internet and into the virtual library. One survey of 400 colleges discovered that two-thirds of the institutions had incidents of sexual harassment by computer; 60 percent reported that student computer accounts had been used without permission; half found damage or menacing acts by hackers; and 37 percent said that students had been the victims of electronic hate messages. In half of the schools, students had downloaded pornographic words or pictures into the computers in their dormitory rooms (Electronic harassment, 1998). Most academic libraries that offer graphical access to the Web through their online systems are dealing with these same problems. While students must sign an Acceptable Use Policy (AUP) to get an e-mail account on the campus network, they usually do not have to sign one to have access to the library system. Community users likewise present challenges because they do not sign an AUP either. Libraries need policies that protect minors and identify the consequences for system abuse.

A study by researchers at Carnegie Mellon University has identified a statistically significant trend: the more time that the individuals studied spent at their computer terminals, the more depressed and lonely they were at the end of the experiment (Adler, 1998). Despite the many social benefits of the Internet as a means to connect people with each other through e-mail, chat rooms, and discussion groups, excessive use tends to foster social isolation, depression, and loneliness.

Studies by MIT psychologist Sherry Turkle also warn of the dangers of becoming too enamored with computers and the Internet. The language used by technologists has migrated into our daily speech patterns, and "we are learning to see ourselves as plugged-in technobodies" (1995, p. 177). She sees that computer-mediated communication can affect one's ability to relate to other people. Both children and adults who are lonely and isolated like computers because "it can feel like somebody is always there, always ready, always responsive, but without the responsibility of having to deal with another person" (1984, p. 146). Role-playing games such as MUDs are particularly seductive because they allow individuals to live in cyberspace with a persona that may be more interesting and satisfying than the one in real life.

Research on Internet and computer use has implications for libraries as a warning for librarians to monitor the behavior of frequent users who may monopolize a terminal in a public lab or those staff who may seem to be growing more withdrawn as they work. Ideally, each job should have a variety of tasks so that staff can get away from terminals for an adequate amount of time to have physical movement. Staff who seem to spend excessive amounts of time "playing on the Internet" need to be counseled about job productivity and responsibility. To a large extent the need to subscribe to professional listservs has added to the responsibility of reviewing professional literature and staying current in the field. The dilemma is that more time is required to scan through hundreds of messages to determine which are useful, which should be saved or printed, and which can be deleted. Some staff need a minimum of two hours per day just to keep up with their e-mail, and this can have a negative impact on time management and productivity.

Postman (1992, p. 114) cautions against viewing computers or machines as having human attributes, and conversely expecting people to perform like machines. He questions the value of automating processes for efficiency when the more appropriate question is whether the processes are necessary or important.

Some corporations have developed policies prohibiting use of the Internet and e-mail during specified hours in order to curb the loss of productivity. Software monitors are also available which report the time each employee spends online. Such "big brother" approaches impinge on individual privacy and contribute to a hostile working environment. Ideally, staff should be able to contribute to the expectation of the job and discuss the relationship of Internet use and productivity with their supervisors.

Choosing Our Future

Asking the big-picture questions of a midlife crisis is an appropriate way to begin to plan where we go from here: What are we doing? What should we be doing? What should we be doing next? What should we not be doing? Next, we should pursue strategic questions that identify environmental conditions, competitors, and possible partners. Create a list of values that are important to your organization. Tennant advises us "to talk with experts in other professions, read nonlibrary journals, and query users. We need to think imaginatively, by first throwing out our common assumptions and frames of reference and then brainstorming possible solutions" (1998, p. 33).

Recognizing that high technology will only go higher, we can affirm the need for a human response to counterbalance the threat of new technology (Naisbett, 1982, p. 39).

Position the library as a place for people and the organizational center for access to information using appropriate technologies and resources. Identify the mission that everyone can support. Other strategies for success suggested by Boyd (1997) include encouraging experimentation and risk taking; developing the skills of staff; building a team spirit; marketing the library and ourselves as information professionals; continuously evaluating our role and performance; aiming for and expecting the best performance from ourselves and our staff.

The very technologies that have enabled the virtual library have allowed us to provide new services that have been meaningful to users. Nostalgia about the past does not warrant a change of evolutionary course, and I cannot justify returning the Mansell volumes to the space now occupied by five PCs which give access to a seemingly infinite number of electronic resources. The challenges and the opportunity of the present are to choose our future, building on the success and wisdom of the past.

References

Adler, J. (1998). Online and bummed out. *Newsweek, 132* (11), 84.

Balas, J. (1997). Making libraries comfortable. *Computers in Libraries, 17* (8), 49.

Boyd, S. (1997). Evolution and revolution in school library practice. ED 412 951.

Brod, C. (1984). *Technostress: The human cost of the computer revolution.* Reading, MA: Addison-Wesley.

Champion, S. (1988). Technostress: Technology's toll. *School Library Journal, 35,* 48-51.

Clyde, A. (1994). Ergonomics and school library automation. *Emergency Librarian, 22* (1), 52.

Doran, K. (1996). The Internet: Its impact, import, and influence. *Computers in Libraries, 16* (3), 8, 10.

Electronic harassment growing problem in colleges. (1998, January 5). *The Salem Evening News*, p. A2.

Gapen, D. K. (1993). The virtual library: Knowledge, society, and the librarian. In L. M. Saunders (Ed.), *The virtual library: Visions and realities* (pp. 1-14). Medford, NJ: Information Today, Inc.

Healey, J. M. (1998). *Failure to connect: How computers affect our children's minds—for better and worse*. New York: Simon & Schuster.

Keys, M. (1998). Info rage. *The NELINET Liaison, 20* (8), 1, 7.

Metz, R. (1990). The impact of electronic formats and campus networks on university libraries in the United States. *Computers in Libraries, 10* (5), 30-31.

Naisbett, J. (1982). *Megatrends: Ten new directions transforming our lives*. New York: Warner.

Postman, N. (1992). *Technopoly: The surrender of culture to technology*. New York: Vintage Books.

Schuyler, M. (1997). When does filtering turn into censorship? *Computers in Libraries, 17* (5), 34-38.

Tennant, R. (1998). The banal barriers. *Library Journal, 123* (1), 33.

Tenopir, C. (1997). Taking online interaction for granted. *Library Journal, 122* (20), 39-40.

Turkle, S. (1995). *Life on the screen: Identity in the age of the Internet*. New York: Simon & Schuster.

Turkle, S. (1984). *The second self: Computers and the human spirit*. New York: Simon & Schuster.

Von Wahlde, B. (1993). The impact of the virtual library on library management and organization. In Helal, A.H. and Weiss, J. W. (Eds.), *Opportunity 2000: Understanding and serving users in an electronic library*. (pp. 28-41). Essen: Universitatsbibliothek Essen.

Weil, M. M. and Rosen, L. D. (1997). *TechnoStress: Coping with technology @ work @home @ play*. New York: Wiley.

Willner, E. (1998). Preparing data for the Web with SGML/XML. *Information Today, 15* (5): 54.

Woodsworth, A. (1998). Learning for a lifetime. *Library Journal, 123* (1), 62.

Mining
Information Networks:
Intranets and Extranets at Work

Judith Field
Senior Lecturer
Library and Information Science Program
Wayne State University
Detroit, Michigan

HISTORICAL VIEW

When we look back at the 1980s, technological advancements seem to have been made, promoted, and adopted at a relatively slow and almost leisurely pace. This was the decade when we saw the closing of card catalogs and the installation of online public access catalogs. The dominant topics of conversation among library directors included various ways to share resources in a time of declining budgets and horror stories about the latest hardware or software crash. Both the failures of computer products and the lack of comfort among the library staff caused consternation especially with the prospect of acquiring still more technology. This was also the decade when libraries established more multitype consortia, including partnerships with medical libraries and law libraries. On the good days, we happily read about the promises of quality and the provision of an all-encompassing customer service that virtual libraries would allow us to provide. We felt assured that the fulfillment of this vision was near at hand. On the bad days when systems had crashed, we generated thoughts that would not have merited a "G" rating.

By the 1990s many of us felt like we were riding a roller coaster which was being driven by the continuous improvements being made in computer hardware and software. Online public access catalogs (OPACs) had become prevalent, and CD-ROM products showed great promise as reliable storage and retrieval products. The Internet was promoted as a free information tool available to everyone. Technologists promised great things, but librarians who visited the Internet were initially dismayed by the chaotic access paths to locate useful information.

The greatest potential for library applications seemed to be e-mail, discussion groups, and formalized listservs as ways to get reference help and to do troubleshooting. Concurrently, library association annual conferences, other information conferences, and continuing education courses promoted and offered a variety of programs on how to telnet, transfer files, and locate useful sites on the Internet. Articles and books touting the viability of the Internet became available. The actual day-to-day problems encountered in libraries made many of the assertions of vendors sound like pie-in-the-sky. Even the professional articles that touted the arrival of virtual libraries seemed to be based on fantasy rather than on reality. Commercial online database providers still seemed to be the most dependable resource for current, timely, and comprehensive information.

Every few months improved computers and software products were introduced to the market. The rapid introductions of these new products made it hard to decide which platforms to adopt. The good news was the fact that the computers, and the networks that used them, became more reliable, making the dreams of a virtual library more attainable. The development of efficient browsers accelerated this movement to the Internet. More and more people, not just librarians, started to mount information on the Internet and use it as an information resource. Academic and public libraries created networks in their regions, making any library the place to go to determine what was available in the area. This was then carried to the next step when more individuals started to access these computers from their own homes. If you eavesdropped on conversations in elevators or in the cafeteria, you could hear people talking about what libraries they had browsed the night before and what information resources they had found. Nightly news programs had stories on the Internet and how it was being used, and using a computer to find a new information site was starting to become a case of one-upsmanship. Peter Drucker (1993) declared that the Knowledge Age had arrived, and everybody—from small children to senior citizens—wanted to be a player.

By the mid-1990s improved browsers and the growing media attention in news stories and advertising made the Internet the place everyone wanted to be. The time had finally come when libraries could actually provide service twenty-four hours a day and seven days a week to anyone who dialed into their sites. This new access and the restrictions of commercial database licenses meant that they had to develop new policies and procedures for collection usage and revise collection development policies that no longer fit the new environment. New job responsibilities included the design and maintenance of Web pages and the development and implementation of methodologies for constantly evaluating the contents of Web pages. Additionally, librarians became skilled trainers in order to assist their customers in successfully surfing the Internet and efficiently troubleshooting their systems. This new electronic environment brought access issues dealing with censorship back to the forefront, particularly in the matter of Internet filters for school and public libraries.

SPECIAL LIBRARIANS

During this period special librarians also experimented with the Internet, initially seeing the prime advantage of the Internet as a communication device with other colleagues. This included participating in topical listservs like buslib-l. For doing research, commercial databases remained their primary information resource. They knew the advantages and shortcomings of each database, and they could rely on them to provide quality and timely information for their clients. At conferences like the Special Libraries Association, Medical Library Association, American Association of Law Librarians, Computers in Libraries, the National Online Meeting, and Online, they learned how to use the Internet by taking continuing education courses from the early adopters in the field like Hope Tillman from Babson College.

The reorganization, reengineering, downsizing, and outsourcing waves that organizations went through in the late 1980s also had an impact on special librarians. As a result of these movements, libraries had fewer staff, less physical space, greater demands for services, and an increased pressure for accountability. Acquisition of CD-ROM products served as both a space saving solution and a way to reduce online search costs. Another strategy was to reevaluate the Internet as an information resource. Special librarians were assisted in this evaluation activity by working in partnership with the corporate MIS department. Most MIS departments promoted internal networks called Intranets. The key issues that needed to be considered in implementing these networks were security, connectivity, reliability, productivity, and the supposed need for constant upgrades. The potential for installing these secured networks showed a lot of promise, and special librarians made themselves part of the solution.

INTRANETS

By the end of 1995 Intranets started to become more evident within those American corporations that considered the ability to access and share information as a strategy for increasing employee productivity. As MIS departments continued to promote the latest in management systems, it became clear that librarians could play a major role in developing the content which would create successful Intranets.

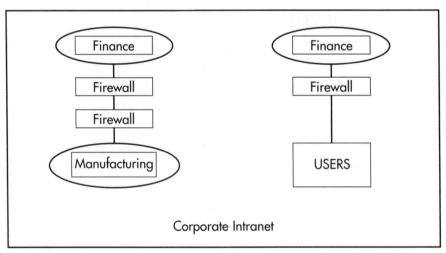

Figure 2.1

So, what is an Intranet? (See Figure 2.1.) The Internet is a network of networks consisting of thousands of public networks, each of which is interconnected. An Intranet, on the other hand, is a private or proprietary network which can be accessed only by a specific audience, usually an organization's employees or members. Sections of the Intranet may only be available to select departments, such as personnel. Outsiders are barred access to an organization's Intranet by a firewall.

Intranets are designed to disseminate and retrieve internal corporate information and to serve as the mainstream infrastructure or backbone that supplies such mission critical applications as research projects or the payment of bills. Access to this information is done by digitizing all relevant information decision-making material, from policy and procedure manuals to laboratory notebooks, and mounting them on the Web server. The next step is to design seamless access to this material so that using the Intranet will be intuitive for all employees. Top uses of Intranets are e-mail and employee collaboration on research projects. Other main uses of the Intranet have been document management, scheduling activities, and a central access point for corporate directories.

The development of Intranets has allowed librarians to take a visible role in providing access to an organization's intellectual capital. In fact, Intranets have allowed us to show our professional and personal competencies, such as those listed in the Special Libraries Association's publication, *Competencies for Special Librarians of the 21st Century*. These competencies can be mastered by all librarians and information professionals and include the follow roles:

- Identifier of critical information
- Organizer of information for access
- Packager of the information
- Disseminator of the information

These competencies can be applied to the creation of effective Web pages, which employees can access. These Web pages should also be considered marketing tools for the services that the library offers. It is this easy accessibility to desired information that will encourage employees to rely on the Intranet as a reliable source to aid them in doing their jobs effectively. To facilitate this, librarians need to work closely with senior administration to develop a knowledge management system which is a true resource sharing system and not just a top-down communication device. Working with senior administration will also ensure that the library has support from all departments to mount their current documents and to adopt procedures for reviewing material for which they are responsible. This knowledge management system should be designed to foster increased productivity, whether the organization's work force is on the road, working from home, or working beyond regular working hours.

The initial design of the system must incorporate a security program that identifies which employees have complete or partial access to designated files that are on the organization's Intranet. This hierarchical access must be carefully designed in conjunction with the department heads and the MIS department. One of the decisions that will be made at this juncture is what groupware is to be utilized on the network. Some common groupware, like LotusNotes or grapeVINE, may already be in use by one or more departments. The structure of the Intranet and the way it can be accessed mimic many operational aspects of the Internet. While individuals searching on the Internet justifiably have concerns about the privacy of transactions, security in the Intranet environment is built in and carefully monitored so competitors cannot access critical information.

While librarians can help structure the knowledge management system, they must continue to fulfill information requests. Some of these requests can be handled by identifying relevant Internet sites for people to consult. Employees can identify these by consulting the library's Web page for hotlinks to reliable Internet sites. This access to the external world is provided by going through a secured portal. Use of the Internet to get information will continue to increase as more of the commercial online database firms mount Web products. Just as CD-ROM products were not identical to the print products that they supplanted, the same can also be said for the current versions of the commercial database Web products. Some of the criticisms at this time are that they are slower to access and search; their search capabilities are more limited; many of the databases seem less complete; they are not as easy to download, format, or print; and the current interfaces are harder to use. These differences are important to note because most of our end users are not sophisticated searchers. West Group is one of the companies that introduced a product called "West Intranet Toolkit" at the American Association of Law Librarians in July 1998 to deal with some of these issues. Other companies are also developing better Web search tools.

Providing access to various commercial databases is just one way that librarians can enrich the content of their Intranet site. Another way is to identify research projects, develop profiles, and send the latest information regularly to particular researchers. One can do this by sending executive summaries related to specific research or by developing an electronic newsletter to share more general information. This needs to be done carefully since researchers are also dealing with information overload. Any automatic profile programs must be designed appropriately and reviewed at regular intervals. Librarians will quickly be able to identify those who want full-text information on relevant topics and those who want brief extracts with the option of getting the full article at another time. Another critical service that librarians can offer is training employees on how to use the system, providing self-training modules on their portion of the Web site, and monitoring access and usage of specific segments of the Intranet. One complication is that not all employees will be on site, so creative methods must be employed to train those at remote locations. Some of these employees may be using different platforms, so the MIS department may need to provide assistance. To personalize services, librarians can still use the telephone or try any available video conferencing technologies which enable users to talk one-to-one or to present to a group with two-way interaction.

There are many success stories about librarians who have implemented effective Intranets. Each of these success stories shows how librarians have restructured their services to more closely align the library with the goals and objectives of their organization. The Boeing Technical Library is an example of a special library that developed a "Strategic-Target-Process" otherwise known as S-T-P. This received the endorsement of Boeing's Administrative Services Quality Council. This honor labeled the library as the external information process owner, which they then combined with their ongoing role of making the external Web more accessible. Their efforts increased the credibility of all library personnel as skilled managers of information. The Owens Corning Library in Cincinnati, Ohio, is another model. Director Nancy Lemon provides library services through an electronic virtual environment, increasing the visibility of her staff.

Cases like these demonstrate that librarians can take the initiative in creating knowledge tools deliverable to the desktop. Intranets allow librarians to stretch and be creative in designing information services. Even working in a small organization as a solo librarian, one can take advantage of the opportunities provided by developing an Intranet. Librarians who are not familiar with Intranets might look for additional publications or a seminar offered in conjunction with a professional conference.

EXTRANETS

The term Extranet was first coined in 1996. The concept was a natural evolution as resource sharing and cost containment became the way to make a profit. An Extranet is essentially a private wide area network that runs on the public protocols of the Internet. It can also be defined as a hybrid that combines features of the Internet and Intranets. It is designed to enable partners, suppliers, and customers to share information with an organization. Each supplier or partner is able to access clearly defined resources by using a password and encryption for reading communications. This does not allow for full penetration into the organization's Intranet. The passwords or authorization codes that people are given allow them to enter through one firewall while the organization's Intranet is still protected by another firewall. For organizations this means fewer sales calls since their suppliers can determine the quantity of product available and automatically generate an order to be approved. Web access enables customer service to deal with questions and problems and build good will.

Extranet Web pages can be very effective marketing devices. Associations are also using Extranets to market their services and are creating "member-only" sections which can only be accessed by password or membership number. Extranets are not just for corporate America or for professional associations—academic libraries and public libraries are also developing them. One site to monitor is the Extranet at the Hennepin County Library in Minnesota. Obviously a critical issue here is security, and these sites need to be monitored on a regular basis to insure that no competitive information is being accessed or distributed, or licensing agreement broken.

Corporate librarians are charged with providing information resources to a carefully defined user group. As organizations become more virtual with the aid of technology, and more global due to mergers, or the demand for their product goes international, librarians will find themselves providing information services to a more disparate user group. One new role is to make sure that the material designated to be shared is not confidential or that it is not under copyright. There should be procedures in place to mark confidential company documents. Unfortunately the ease of creating attachments and printing makes it very easy to share copyrighted material. Rules need to be in place so that the librarian can have the authorization to pull material which violates the copyright law or company acceptable use procedures.

The Extranet also allows the library to provide information as a good will gesture to a valued supplier or customer. While requests should be handled on a one-to-one basis, librarians must exercise great sensitivity in handling these requests. Library service priorities must be clear so that the primary responsibilities are not neglected or conflicts created while providing services to people who are not part of the immediate organization. Librarians should volunteer to help design the external Web pages to be sure that their access directions are intuitive. They should also serve as one of the designated monitors who regularly audit the content of the Web pages for both content and currency. At the same time they should also verify that all links are working. Applications for the Extranet are just being developed. Three examples are mentioned here:

- Collaboration: The Extranet can push the ability to collaborate to a new level, allowing employees in the same department or different areas to work together simultaneously on a single document, and to allow customers, suppliers, or competitors to participate as appropriate.
- Push Technology: Extranets can also support "Push Technology," but this must be carefully implemented so that people do not suffer from information overload to the extent that they feel that this service is intrusive, violates their privacy, or impacts their productivity.
- Conferencing: Extranets can utilize the audio and video transmission capabilities that are enabled on the Internet, saving the time and costs associated with face-to-face meetings.

A LIBRARIAN'S REFLECTIONS

The virtual interactive environment offers librarians interesting challenges as we continue to be recognized as key information providers. We have only five years of experience incorporating this technology into our work. Changes are still coming, but many librarians feel that it will be more of the same—though the tools will be faster and more reliable. The Internet has changed the way we learn, work, conduct our personal affairs, and entertain ourselves. It is becoming an integral part of our daily lives, and the reliance on technology is rapidly increasing.

As librarians, we need to align ourselves with our organization's core business. We should reflect on how our organizations have changed due to external forces and ask how the library has likewise changed. This is necessary for public and academic librarians as well as special librarians. Because the new virtual environment permits the decentralization of functions, we are challenged to retain our identity as the organization's key information provider.

In order to successfully meet these challenges of the changing information environment, we must continue our professional growth by taking the following steps:

- Take continuing education courses offered by the library associations
- Enroll in relevant classes at nearby colleges
- Attend subject specific conferences like Internet Librarian, Online, or Computers in Libraries
- Broaden your reading to include technical and industry specific literature
- Participate in video conferences like the Special Libraries Association program on Intranets
- Subscribe and participate in listservs, allowing your colleagues to be part of your brain trust

The twenty-first century is going to be an exciting one for the information profession. Globalization is going to continue, the Internet and its related networks are going to become more pervasive. The current worries of security and downtime will not go away, but the dependability of these networks will equal the reliability of our public utilities. Data, information, and knowledge will continue to grow at a geometric rate. The downside of this is that data, information, and knowledge is not created equal, and artificial intelligence agents will not soon replace the keen insight that a librarian brings to the selection or process. This is the time for you to step forward with new and creative ideas on how to make the technology work for your clientele.

Recommended Resources

David, H. (1997, August). The extranet team play. *Internet World, 8*, 56.

Drucker, P. (1993, Spring). The rise of the knowledge society. *Wilson Quarterly, 17*, 52-70.

Gareiss, R. (1997, June). Industrial strength extranet. *Data Communications, 26*, 70-74.

Intranet Professional (May/June 1998- v1 n1-).

Knowledge management: A new competitive asset. (1998). Washington, DC: Special Libraries Association.

Lemon, N. (1996, November/December). Climbing the value chain. *Online, 20*(6), 20, 50.

Mace, S. (1997, December). The extranet revolution. *Byte, 22*, 65-92.

Mullich, J. (1998, June 1). An extranet built to last. *PC Week, 15*(22), 33.

Product services: Strategies for information services (1996, April/May). *Bulletin of the American Society for Information Science, 22* (4), 15-16.

Starnes, J. K., Graves, J. & Justice, J. (1997). *The complete intranet source for information professionals.* Washington, DC: Special Libraries Association.

The virtual workplace: One size doesn't fit all. (1997). Washington, DC: Special Libraries Association.

Volgman, K. W. (1998, July). Instant information access: Redefining the workplace. *IIE Solutions, 30*(7), 36.

Zorn, P. (1997, May/June). Surfing corporate intranets: Search tools that control the undertow. *Online, 21*, 30.

Building a Digital Library:
The Stories of the Making of America

Maria S. Bonn, Ph.D.
Interface Specialist, Digital Library Production Service
University of Michigan
Ann Arbor, Michigan

The University of Michigan Making of America (MoA) (http://www/umdl.
umich.edu/moa) is a digital library of primary sources in American social history from the antebellum period through reconstruction. It was born out of a major collaborative endeavor between the University of Michigan and Cornell University, initially funded by the Andrew W. Mellon Foundation. This effort aimed to preserve and make accessible through digital technology a significant body of primary sources in United States history. MoA also seeks to develop protocols for the selection, conversion, storage, retrieval, and use of digitized materials on a large, distributed scale.

The University of Michigan MoA collection is a collaborative effort within the University Library, involving staff from Collection Development, Preservation, Technical Services, and the Digital Library Initiative. Primary responsibility for the production of the MoA system lies with the Digital Library Production Service (DLPS) (http://www.umdl.umich.edu). The University of Michigan collection contains approximately 1,600 books and 50,000 journal articles with nineteenth-century imprints, a total of over 630,000 pages. The selection of materials for inclusion focused on monographs in the subject areas of education, psychology, American history, sociology, religion, science and technology, and periodicals of literary and general interest. These texts were chosen through a process in which subject-specialist librarians worked with faculty in a variety of disciplines to identify materials that will be most readily applicable to research and teaching needs.

The Making of America has enjoyed enormous success both within the scholarly community and with the general public. User reception of the searchable pages available at the site has been overwhelmingly positive: materials previously unused and in storage are now being searched as many as 120,000 times a month, and users are displaying more than 75,000 pages each month. Further, other institutions have begun to adopt the University of Michigan deployment strategy in their preservation efforts. MoA serves as a model for conversion that accommodates both automatically processed and carefully prepared (proofread and fully encoded) materials, where journals can coexist with monographs, and where preservation and access are equally well supported. The MoA system is not only extremely well received by users but is also being embraced as a model by other institutions, such as members of the Digital Library Federation (DLF).[1]

MoA is extensively used, both by users the developers anticipated and by those we did not. MoA has been used in history classrooms at the University of Michigan and at other institutions and faculty and graduate students from all over the country use the collection for their research. Scholars at the *Oxford English Dictionary* use MoA to search for earliest uses of words. In addition, MoA has seen significant use from more surprising audiences, such as genealogists, hobbyists, and literary societies.

The breadth of uses and users of MoA has been one of the more surprising and rewarding aspects of the project. As the developers originally anticipated, MoA is an electronic research repository serving historical scholars and as such is part of the academic library context out of which it grew. But because of its appeal to the general public, it also serves another mission. This broad, valuable, freely available collection serves as a public digital library, providing useful and interesting materials to patrons of all backgrounds and levels of expertise.

At this point, reading about a digital collection in a paper volume, perhaps far from your Internet connection, you may well be asking, "But what does it let me *do?*" It lets you do many different things: You can find materials on premature burial, the *code duello,* phrenology, and "fancy fairs" with simple phrase searching. You can compare the collocation of the words "virtue" and "vice" near "poverty" in articles in nineteenth-century journals. You can put together a bibliography of abolitionist tracts or look at illustrations from reports on explorations by the United States Army Corps of Engineers. In short, MoA gives you the ability to search thousands of pages of full text very quickly and in a number of ways. The sample screen images that accompany this article give examples of some of the possibilities for uses of MoA, as well as the flavor of the materials in the system. (See Figures 3.1, 3.2, 3.3, 3.4.)

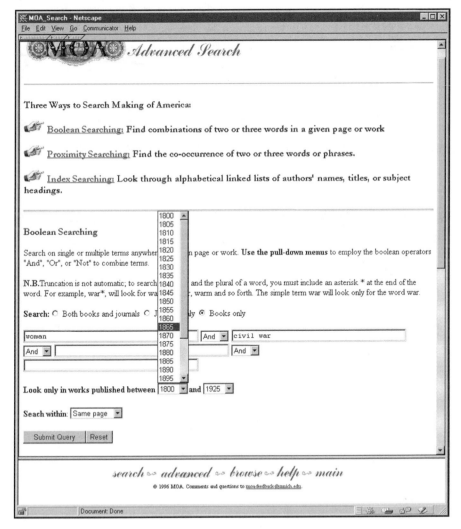

Figure 3.1   Boolean search interface: Note the restrictions that are available with the search.

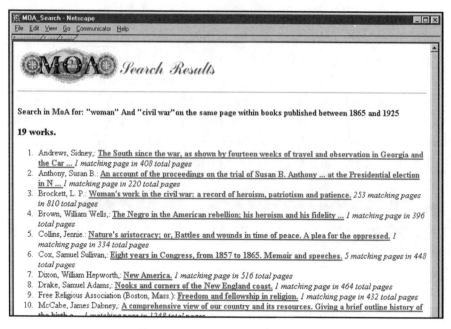

Figure 3.2   Sample results page/hit list with feedback on density of results.

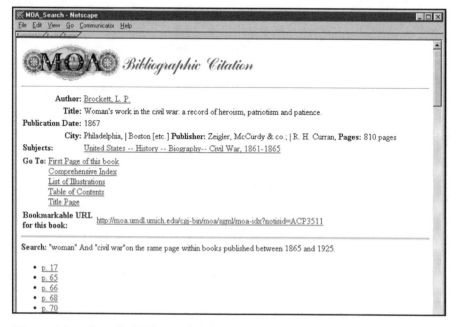

Figure 3.3   Sample bibliographic header with links to special pages and to location of search results.

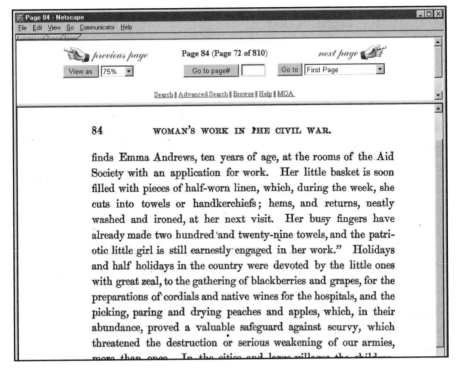

Page 84 - Netscape

Figure 3.4   Page image and navigational frame.

THE STORIES OF THE MAKING OF AMERICA

The story of the development of the Making of America collection is not a single linear narrative. Instead it is a collection of stories that have a common focus but very different points of view. There is a genealogical story that traces the attempts to build a stable coalition of institutions dedicated to the project and of negotiation and collaboration and the productive tension between the aims of preservation and access. There is an architectural history of the building of a digital collection that will be able to grow into a true digital library, not simply remain a special collection. And within that there is a technical report detailing the methods for creating a viable and sustainable online system with a high degree of functionality and the possibility of scaling to accommodate future growth. Although this discussion cannot do justice to the complexity of all those stories (and there are no doubt others to be told as well), it hopes to suggest some of the key points of all three.

A PROJECT GENEALOGY

The Making of America was initially conceived as a multi-institutional partnership with emphasis on the digital conversion of monographs. In an early and ambitious iteration the project partners proposed the staged conversion and deployment of 100,000 volumes from a 100-year period (1850-1950). From early exploratory discussions to the initial work on conversion and deployment, the project went through a three-year period of definition, refinement, and negotiation among possible partner institutions, as well as active fund seeking. In the end, the Making of America emerged as a project with firm commitments from the University of Michigan and Cornell University and with funding from the Mellon Foundation.

Cornell and Michigan shared a common set of goals in their development of the MoA collection. The collection was built to facilitate large-scale preservation of nineteenth-century American materials. Within that aim, the institutions wished to base the collection on a clearly articulated and intellectually viable *selection* process, to create an efficient *conversion* process, to build a functional *access* system, and to create a system that could undergo *evaluation* through actual use. Although the institutions began from this common point, they brought to the project different histories and experiences with digital projects. These experiences led to differing emphases within the goals and differing outcomes in the development of the MoA systems.

In a number of significant early efforts, Cornell demonstrated the value of being able to scan and print preservation-quality images. In efforts involving materials such as mathematical monographs, Cornell was able to create print replacement copies while storing valuable digital surrogates. In light of this successful earlier experience, in the MoA project Cornell continued to focus its energy on the specifications and quality control of the conversion process and page image production.

The University of Michigan brought to MoA a history of creating full text access to digital materials. In the TULIP project and in UMLibText, the University of Michigan Library had already created a number of successful methods for searching and displaying text in digital form (Lougee, 1998). Work done at the University of Michigan for the JSTOR project had also demonstrated the value of marrying preservation standards and access strategies of OCR and indexing (Guthrie & Lougee, 1997). Added to this was the expertise of the University of Michigan Humanities Text Initiative in dealing with monographic materials. Building upon this combination of experiences, the University of Michigan was able to commit itself to creating a highly functional access system that allowed fast searching, retrieval of relevant pages, and access to both bibliographic and full-text information, as well as more conventional page turning and browsing mechanisms.

These divergent paths have led to quite different outcomes in the systems. Cornell has produced a significant number of replacement volumes for the items it disbound for the MoA collection. At present it provides online access to a sample of the journal volumes it has converted. These volumes are navigated by browsing the tables of contents of the original volumes and using a "go to page" mechanism to locate a desired article. The University of Michigan Library has embraced a different model; while not putting a premium on reprints (the University of Michigan anticipates making reprints in the future only on demand), it has put online the entire body of its converted materials and built a system that allows a variety of ways of accessing and navigating the materials.

In the end, Cornell and University of Michigan decided to at least temporarily eschew the difficulties of creating a fully integrated system. The two institutions shared a procurement process and have communicated about their plans and methods for online implementation. They have remained committed to facilitating searching across the two collections. Cornell has recently made a decision to adopt the University of Michigan access model and has contracted with DLPS for the OCR of their page images and for implementation of an access system. When this process is complete, the partner institutions can move back to a vision of an integrated collection. After an extended period of independent exploration and development, the two efforts hope to come back together in mutually enriching ways.

An Architectural History: Building a Special Collection into a Digital Library

Like most full-text collections available on the World Wide Web, MoA is thematically focused. The building of such online collections has led to a number of high quality and carefully constructed scholarly resources. Where MoA differs from these collections, however, is in its size and its ability to grow even larger. The mass of the content and the scalability of the system are the key features that will allow MoA to grow out of being a special project into a true digital library. As this growth happens, we hope to better understand how we can apply our existing knowledge about libraries to online systems and about the continuities and discontinuities in user behavior as users move from physical to electronic stacks.

MoA hopes to promote a productive and dynamic synergy between a relatively new and developing system architecture for *digital libraries* and an established intellectual architecture for *libraries*. The system architecture of MoA has three guiding principles. First, we are intent on developing a system that can accommodate further treatment of the materials (such as full encoding) and better access processes, as they become available. Second, there is a strong commitment to a system that can scale as we include more materials. We hope to add thousands of volumes to the system in the next few years, and the access and delivery mechanisms must be able to grow with the content. Finally, we are committed to a high degree of usability. We facilitate behavior that is consistent with the existing use of paper journals and monographs, aiming to make the digital copies an acceptable surrogate for the print counterpart.

Our understanding of how people use these texts—and our vision of the whole MoA system—comes, to a high degree, out of the professional and intellectual experience of librarianship. MoA was built by library staff: the bulk of the programming, the system design, the management of OCR processes, and the interface development were all carried out by professional librarians working with library staff in the more traditional areas of collection development, preservation, and cataloging. We have aimed to bring together technical expertise with our training in and understanding of information organization, collection development, and research needs. Moreover, we have drawn upon existing library standards for comprehensive and varied collections and commitment to broad public service. By doing so, we hope to make MoA a model digital library that reflects the best principles of the traditional library.

Not only do we aim to make MoA a digital library in *conception,* but we also look for it to work as a library in *use.* By seeding MoA with substantial content, by pursuing opportunities for growth, and by facilitating a number of access strategies, we seek to simulate the experience of research in the library stacks. Users can conduct finely targeted searches—they can also browse and play. They can search on subject headings. They can work closely with individual volumes, or they can get a sense of the coverage within a period on a particular subject. There is enough material that anyone interested in the period can return repeatedly for different purposes and find useful texts. To a large degree we have tried to support such variety of use by not over-anticipating types of use. We aimed to build as large a collection as was feasible given our resources; we thought about research behavior and how to facilitate it, without being overly deterministic. Actual use of MoA has shown us that users are more creative and ingenious than we could ever have imagined. Like a physical academic library, we have had to work on maintaining a sense of balance: between dedication to defined primary users (e.g., "research faculty") with serving the general public (e.g., "citizens of the state of Michigan") and between anticipating user needs and avoiding limiting the possibilities for use of the material.

TECHNICAL NOTES: METHODS FOR CREATING A SCALABLE AND SUSTAINABLE ONLINE SYSTEM

The previous section details some of the theory that went into the design of MoA. The success of the implementation also depends, of course, on a set of practices that make that theory realizable. What follows are brief descriptions of some of the methods that make MoA work.

SELECTION

At Michigan, collection specialist librarians gave the Systems Office a set of criteria (date range, United States imprint, materials that had been removed to remote storage) and asked the office to generate lists of titles that met those criteria. The subject specialists then went through the lists, marking likely looking titles. Hourly staff moved the selected volumes from remote storage to the specialist's office for review and final selection. Special collections had the option of reviewing all volumes before the texts were sent on into the conversion process.

The thematic focus of the initial phase—antebellum period through reconstruction, 1850-1877—was chosen for several reasons. First, scholarly and general interest in this period of American history remains high, thus increasing the potential of the collection to support the research and teaching needs of the partner institutions. Second, much of the literature of this period is deteriorating rapidly and to preserve it the materials must be refor-matted—the materials were already high priority preservation candidates. Third, the body of literature is of a manageable size so a cohesive collection in digital form could be assembled quickly. Finally, the publications from this period are not covered by copyright protection and thus can be made freely available to the public.

As MoA continues to grow, the developers hope to move toward a more automatic method for identifying materials for conversion. By establishing and using broad selection criteria (for example, *all* volumes within a certain date and imprint range that are currently housed in remote storage), rather than making volume by volume decisions, we hope to considerably reduce the time and effort of selection.

CONVERSION

The materials in the MOA collection are scanned from the original paper source. The volumes were disbound—the texts were often so brittle and dam-aged that this had to take place locally rather than risking destruction in ship-ping. (After scanning, all pages were returned and are now stored in preserva-tion boxes in the remote storage facility, pending a final decision about their disposition).[2] A service vendor did the scanning itself. The images are captured at 600 dpi in TIFF image format and compressed using CCITT Group 4. Minimal document structuring occurs at the point of conversion, primarily link-ing image numbers to pagination and tagging self-referencing portions of the text, such as indices and tables of contents. In the case of serials, low-level indexing was added post-conversion by the partner institutions; Cornell and Michigan staff collaborated to determine low-level indexing guidelines for this complex group of serial titles (Shaw & Blumson, 1997).

The MoA images also went through a quality control process when they came back from the service vendor. Making this process efficient proved to be an important lesson of the project. Originally, the images were loaded into our system and processed, including the OCR, as soon as they arrived from the vendor. The Preservation Department then checked each image for acceptable clarity and degree of skew. If images were rejected by Preservation, they were returned to the vendor, and we waited for them to come back through our process again. This caused extensive duplication of effort, which consumed a great deal of time, and it did not allow communication with the vendor early enough to correct systemic problems. In the future, any substantial additions to MoA will pass through quality control *first*. Preservation will review a statistically determined sample of the images and either reject or accept batches of images. When the images have passed through quality control, they will then only have to be loaded and processed once.

ACCESS

Once the page images were returned to the University of Michigan, DLPS conducted fully automated OCR to generate the searchable text for the system. Additional processing cleaned up some basic problems with the OCR (non-ASCII characters) and converted bibliographic metadata into a TEI conformant header.

A commitment to flexibility and extensibility was central to the development of the OCR process. When improved OCR technology is developed, as has happened twice since the inception of the first project, the materials can be treated again at very little cost. Further, high priority items can be moved through a process where the OCR is fully corrected, and the text fully encoded. This is an expensive process but adds functionality (e.g., chapter navigation or display of encoded text in addition to images) and can be applied selectively as resources and demands allow.

Since the completion of the most recent OCR process, the Digital Library Production Service at the University of Michigan has conducted an analysis of the accuracy of the OCR and the confidence ratings assigned by the OCR software. The goal of this project was to develop a method for distinguishing accurate OCR files from OCR files with an unacceptable number of errors, without having to examine each file. This ability will enable the Digital Library Production Service to put online those OCR files with a high probability of accuracy and to estimate the amount of "clean-up" required to correct pages with an unacceptable number of errors (see Bicknese, 1998).

Another important aspect of the MoA system is the method of page image delivery. As indicated above, the MoA images are stored in TIFF format. TIFF, however, is not a format that is widely understood by World Wide Web browsers. Because of this, page images that are presented to the user are converted to GIF format, which is universally understood. This is facilitated by the use of Tif2gif, a specialized utility which converts TIFF images to GIF images quickly, but with a limited set of scaling options. Tif2gif, written by Doug Orr, was originally developed at the University of Michigan and is used in a variety of our digital collections (Shaw & Blumson, 1997). As John Price-Wilkin (1997) has pointed out, there are two important rationales for making the material available through dynamic rather than precomputed and stored transformations: "First, we assume that the patterns of use in our collections mirror those of traditional libraries, where many of the materials go unused for significant periods of time, and where many resources are used only once in an extended period of time. Consequently, creating derivatives for potential use will result in most derivatives being unused and both computational and human resources being wasted." Second, this method also ensures flexibility and the possibility of forward migration in the system. It makes the quick and widespread delivery of the page images possible in the present and allows for the possibility of better delivery in the future. As better delivery strategies are developed, we can return to the original high quality images and adapt their presentation to these better methods.

Future Directions for the Making of America

The development phase of Making of America ended in 1997 (periods of assessment and refinement are part of the ongoing work of MoA), and MoA has been in full production and use for over a year. MoA is, however, very much a work in progress, and the developers are committed to adding both to the content and functionality of the system. Our immediate goals include the following:

- We will further integrate the Making of America materials at Cornell University (http://moa.cit.cornell.edu/).
- Text will gradually migrate from raw OCR to fully corrected and encoded text, based on the availability of resources and specific demands. The Humanities Text Initiative, a part of DLPS at the University of Michigan, will undertake the process of proofing OCR and refining markup based on user demand. The HTI, as part of its American Verse Project (http://www.hti.umich.edu/english/amverse) is currently in the process of encoding over 200 volumes of poetry from the MoA collection.

- The University of Michigan Library will be incorporating digital conversion into its Preservation Department's "Brittle Books" program. New materials will be added to the MoA site as they are converted.
- We are working with other institutions and funding agencies to make more significant additions to the MoA site.

One substantial measure of our success in building MoA will be whether we have indeed designed a system that has room to grow and that can accommodate and facilitate these goals.

MoA is a complex system. Designing and building a complex system is a complex process. As these brief stories may illustrate, it takes significant efforts to find funding, to build coalitions between and within libraries, to define standards, to undertake the conversion, and to specify and implement the system. MoA also requires an ongoing commitment to user support, to periodic assessment, and to maintenance and upgrading. Those are a lot of trees to keep track of. But we still need to keep looking at the forest as well. It is valuable for both the system developers and those who would learn from our experience to periodically remind ourselves of what we are trying to do. At the University of Michigan Digital Library Production Service in general, and in MoA in particular, we are trying to build sustainable and usable systems for putting library content online—systems that can grow with growth in our expertise and technological capability and can grow with users as they become more comfortable and experienced with using online texts. In the Making of America, we are designing a system to help preserve an intellectual history that is in danger of being lost and to make accessible that history in powerful ways.

Acknowledgments

The Making of America has from its inception been a highly collaborative effort, and this attempt to summarize some of its history and methods is no less so. I am particularly indebted to conversations with and documents prepared by Wendy Lougee, Assistant Director for Digital Library Initiatives at the University of Michigan, and John Price-Wilkin, Head, Digital Library Production Service, University of Michigan, as well as current and former staff of the Digital Library Production Service, many of whom will hear their voices echoing here.

Notes

1. The Federation was founded by twelve university research libraries and the Library of Congress, the National Archives and Records Administration, the New York Public Library, and the Commission on Preservation and Access. The founding university libraries are California-Berkeley, Columbia, Cornell, Emory, Harvard, Michigan, Pennsylvania State, Princeton, Southern California, Stanford, Tennessee-Knoxville, and Yale. Four additional university libraries have since joined the Federation: Indiana,

Minnesota, and Pennsylvania, and the California Digital Library. The Research Libraries Group (RLG) and the Online Computer Library Center (OCLC) are formal allies of the Federation.

2. It is important not to underestimate the need for staff to move the volumes through the conversion process. At Michigan, this proved a large roadblock and it finally took a group of professional and paraprofessional staff drawn from various parts of the library who were quite literally willing to get their hands dirty to get the project off the ground. These staff put in long hours creating shipping records and packing boxes of volumes to go to the service vendor, and as a consequence of their efforts, the production process was able to begin.

References

Bicknese, D. A. (1998). Measuring the accuracy of the OCR in the making of America. (http://www. umdl.umich.edu/moa/moaocr.html).

Guthrie, K. M. & Lougee, W. P. (1997, February 1). The JSTOR solution: Accessing and preserving the past. *Library Journal 122*, 42-44.

Lougee, W. (1998). The University of Michigan digital library program: A retrospective on collaboration within the academy. *Library Hi Tech, 16*, 51-59.

Price-Wilkin, J. (1997, May). Just-in-time conversion, just-in-case collections: Effectively leveraging rich document formats for the WWW. *D-Lib Magazine.*(http://www.dlib.org/dlib/may97/michigan/ 05pricewilkin.html).

Price-Wilkin, J. & Bonn, M. (1998, September 18). Making of America IV: the American voice, 1850-1876. Proposal submitted to the Andrew W. Mellon Foundation.

Shaw, E. J. & Blumson, S. (1997, July/August). Making of America; Online searching and page presentation at the University of Michigan. *D-Lib Magazine*. (http://www.dlib.org/dlib/july97/america/07shaw.html).

Managing Digital Content:
The Scholarly Communications Project

Gail McMillan
Director, Scholarly Communications and Special Collections
University Libraries
Virginia Polytechnic Institute and State University
Blacksburg, Virginia

The professional literature for library as well as computer science is rich with jargon, and a term currently in vogue is the "digital library." Unfortunately, too many authors write as if a digital library is a database limited to online resources, distinct and separate from a physical library. They ignore the fact that libraries provide user services as well as materials in a variety of media, including digital. For nearly a decade, libraries have not only provided links between users and digital resources; some libraries, like Virginia Tech's, are the originating source of online information. The Scholarly Communications Project (SCP), a department within the University Libraries at Virginia Tech, has nearly ten years of experience in storing and providing access to original electronic works and in designing online systems that improve library services by adapting and enhancing them for the Internet.

BACKGROUND

Since its establishment in 1989, the SCP's goals have been to work with developing Internet technology so that faculty can experiment with new forms of scholarly communication—forms beyond the scope of the academic journal in print, for example. Since then, the SCP has developed the library's electronic reserve system, built and maintained the infrastructure for ejournals and electronic theses and dissertations (ETDs), conceptualized and developed a digital image storage and access system, and worked with regional and international agencies to put timely news reports online.

These and other digital initiatives combine the traditional library focus on collection development and user-friendly services, with a keen awareness and farsightedness that lead to a content-rich future, even when predicting that future in clear detail is not possible. Library services such as those provided through the Scholarly Communications Project support innovative teaching and learning environments while continuing to support traditional classrooms, individual research, and scholarship. This is one way an academic library incorporates digital library operations to serve the university far better than either could independently.

In order to initiate and sustain new forms of scholarship and to support and improve library services for the whole university, University Libraries allocates staff and other resources to the Scholarly Communications Project. It is not enough to accumulate digital resources and provide storage and access systems; SCP also has the responsibility to help users discover and use its resources. SCP staff assist editors, authors, and publishers in putting their works online. Increasingly SCP supports user access to these works through one-on-one contact, including e-mail, telephone, and presentations to workshops and classes.

A compelling need to provide user-friendly services and access dramatically differentiates the traditional library with digital resources from the digital library that may be content rich but service poor. Despite well-designed and implemented computer programs, people still require human interaction. SCP combines rich digital content, automated access and storage systems, and user-friendly library services.

From its inception, SCP staff and committed university faculty have provided the unit's direction. They have collaborated to determine what experiments to conduct, resolved questions arising from the user community, addressed issues raised by the technology, and determined how to meet the needs of users and clients. SCP has grown from a behind-the-scenes and technical support unit into a prominent role as a liaison to students, staff, and faculty who develop and use online resources and services.

ELECTRONIC JOURNALS

One of the initial activities of the SCP was to determine how to publish an electronic journal. By the time the first issue of the *Journal of the International Academy of Hospitality Research* (*JIAHR*) was ready in the fall of 1990, a desktop computer was rigged to be a Gopher server, and *JIAHR* went online as ASCII text. In the ensuing years the SCP migrated this and three more ejournals from Gopher to the Web, and also added another sixteen titles to its roster. Seven are available in multiple electronic formats, most often HTML and PDF. (See Table 4.1.)

Table 4.1	Electronic Journals from the Scholarly Communications Project http://scholar.lib.vt.edu/ejournals			
title	*availability*	*issues online*	*coverage online*	*formats*
ALAN	electronic + paper	11	Winter 1994 -	HTML
Catalyst	electronic + paper	1	Summer 1991-Spring 1995	HTML
CJTCS	electronic only	14	June 1993 -	DVI, PS, PDF
JCAEDE	electronic only	3	Fall 1995-Fall 1997	HTML
JDC	electronic only		Summer 1998 -	HTML
JCN	electronic only	7	May 1996-March 1997	HTML
JFE	electronic + paper	26	1993 -	ASCII
JFLP	electronic only	11	1995 -	DVI, PS
JIAHR	electronic only	9	Nov. 1990 -	HTML
JITE	electronic + paper	13	Fall 1994 -	HTML
JTE	electronic + paper	18	Fall 1989 -	HTML & PDF
JMSEC	electronic + paper	17	1994 -	PS, PDF
JTS	electronic only	4	Summer 1996 -	HTML
JVME	electronic + paper	2	Spring 1997-Fall 1997	HTML
JVTE	electronic + paper	6	Fall 1996 -	HTML
JYSL	electronic + paper	10	Spring 1995-Fall 1997	HTML
Modal	electronic + paper	26	Jan. 1986-Jan. 1993	Bitmaps, HTML
Phil & Tech	electronic only	8	Fall 1995 -	HTML & PDF
SNDE	electronic only	5	Apr. 1996-Apr. 1997	PS, PDF
WILLA	electronic + paper	4	Fall 1992 -	HTML

Eight of SCP's ejournals are the Web equivalents of printed academic journals, enhanced with hot links and twenty-four hour access. Fifteen titles are currently available with three more under development. Forty-five percent are electronic-only journals. All are associated with scholarly societies or professional associations, and four are mirrored for the MIT Press. Four publish individual articles as they complete the peer-review cycles and editorial processes, whereas the remaining thirteen replicate the delays inherent in a traditional academic journal. Only three are not full journals. *The Journal of Fluids Engineering* provides the data that authors have used in the research for their articles published on paper. *The Journal of Youth Services in Libraries* releases tables of contents through the Web, and *Modal Analysis* e-mails abstracts as articles are accepted for publication.

SCP makes it easy for faculty editors to put their journals online by providing them with flexible guidelines (http://scholar.lib.vt.edu/staff/gailmac/ejguide.html). The level of technological expertise among our faculty editors has continued to increase. For example, they no longer want to know which word processor they should use; they want to know if SCP will accept PDF files in addition to HTML. While articles in HTML exist as separate files, our editors prefer that one PDF file contain an entire issue of the journal.

The initial goal of most new ejournal editors is to educate their subscribers. They reason that by publishing online their subscribers have an incentive to use the Internet; then they will navigate to other Web sites and expand to online research. The total number of hits accessing the current full-text ejournals available from SCP increases every year. For example, the volume of access to the *Journal of Technology Education* increased 1,641 percent in 1995, 67 percent in 1996, and 58 percent in 1997. Editors rely on the library to provide the access and archives (including security, appropriate backup, and preservation functions), as well as to support their readers and their students as they branch out to use other online resources.

FACULTY AND STUDENTS BUILD THE DIGITAL LIBRARY

SCP receives almost all of the resources it provides access to in digital format, and this is one reason that the small staff (1.5 FTE), accompanied by a revolving cadre of student assistants, can accomplish so much. The library has not attempted to convert text from hard copy to digital formats on a production scale, nor does it plan to do so. Ejournal editors usually submit new issues as word processed files, and an increasing number are arriving preformatted in HTML or PDF. As needed, SCP students convert ejournal files to Web-friendly displays and link citations to references.

When SCP designed the library's electronic reserve system, we gave faculty various formatting options for making class materials available online. We did not offer, and very few have asked us, to convert print materials to digital formats. There are two reasons for this: digitizing equipment, software, and individual assistance is available in the library; and Virginia Tech faculty also receive equipment, software, and formal training to improve teaching and learning and to create works for the online environment.

The New Media Center (NMC) (http://www.nmc.vt.edu) is a sophisticated and well-staffed computer lab located near the Reference Desk in the main Virginia Tech library. Open to the public, NMC has twenty-one G3/233 MHz Power Macintoshes with PC compatibility and eighteen Apple Color One Scanners, as well as more specialized equipment in an adjacent development lab. Four full-time staff and three FTE student assistants are well trained and have experience with software applications in graphics, desktop publishing, word processing, Web development, 3-D animation, CD-ROM development, digital video, digital audio, and other multimedia areas. Consulting services are available in the NMC, by phone, and at faculty offices.

NMC is used heavily, especially in the summers when the Educational Technology unit conducts intensive faculty training sessions (http://www.fdi. vt.edu/). The Faculty Development Institute (FDI) is part of a university-wide instructional effort to invest in faculty and students by guiding faculty exploration of educational technology. Many FDI participants begin these intensive four-day workshops with little or no experience using computers.

Because Virginia Tech faculty receive training in combination with equipment and software, they are fully prepared to create materials for electronic publication or online classes. Therefore, the library is not seen as a source for converting works to digital formats. The library can devote its resources to storing and delivering content and to mapping traditional services to enhanced, online, user-friendly services. Students seem to learn more independently about new technologies. Since January 1997 Virginia Tech's graduate students have provided another source of digital resources by submitting their masters' theses and doctoral dissertations in electronic formats (see Figure 4.1).

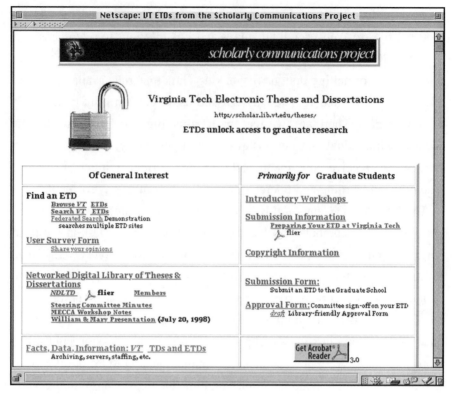

Figure 4.1   ETD Web site at http://scholar.lib.vt.edu/theses/.

Electronic Theses and Dissertations

For decades libraries have stored and infrequently circulated the final product of each graduate student's thesis or dissertation. In 1994 the Virginia Tech Graduate School invited the library to prepare for the inevitable arrival of this research in electronic format. SCP accepted the challenge, developed the procedures and mechanisms for storage and timely access, and created a working prototype. By August 1998 the Networked Digital Library of Theses and Dissertations (NDLTD) included over 1,200 Virginia Tech electronic theses and dissertations (ETDs).

The ETD project is another example of how the library has improved services and increased accessibility to the information for current as well as future users by incorporating digital library resources. The first step was to bring together all the staff involved in processing print theses and dissertations so they could design a parallel workflow for ETDs. Then SCP programmed and enhanced processes to take fuller advantage of the digital resources and the Internet access. For example:

- Students may select unlimited access, university-only access, or no access when they submit their ETDs
- Students and their committee chairs automatically receive e-mail messages with the Internet addresses of their Graduate School approved ETDs
- Users browse or search for ETDs on the Web in addition to the library online catalog much sooner than they would if libraries had to handle paper copies

Virginia Tech is not alone in predicting that initiatives like ETDs provide better library services than do their paper counterparts. In the fall of 1996 the Virginia Tech initiative expanded to include other universities, in part through a grant from the United States Department of Education's Fund for the Improvement of Post-Secondary Education (FIPSE). Currently nearly forty universities in the United States and abroad are also committed to participating in the Networked Digital Library of Theses and Dissertations (http://www.ndltd.org/members/index.htm). Some of their common goals include:

- Collect, catalog, archive, and provide scholars with access to ETDs beyond the host academic community
- Improve timely access to the information within theses and dissertations
- Provide unlimited browsing, searching, and linking to related works and resources on the Internet
- Eliminate the need to bind, stamp, security strip, label, circulate, and reshelve materials so that libraries can serve more users without additional staff
- Reduce the need for additional shelf space in university libraries and archives
- Save students money producing their final research projects
- Allow graduate students to be more creative in documenting their final research
- Enable graduate students to learn about electronic publishing and digital libraries so they gain valuable skills as they complete their degrees

Important to libraries is increasing the size of their digital collections without having to increase the staff to process and maintain the collections (e.g., circulation and reshelving) or the space to house additional works. By archiving and providing access to the digital works of both students and faculty, SCP addresses issues such as online archiving (http://scholar.lib.vt.edu/theses/ archive.html), unrestricted access versus limiting users' access, and intellectual property considerations (http://scholar.lib.vt.edu/theses/copyright/ index.html). Cooperation among separate institutions has also contributed to maximizing access and services as we experiment with simultaneously distributed (i.e., multi-library) and centralized (i.e., single library) searching.

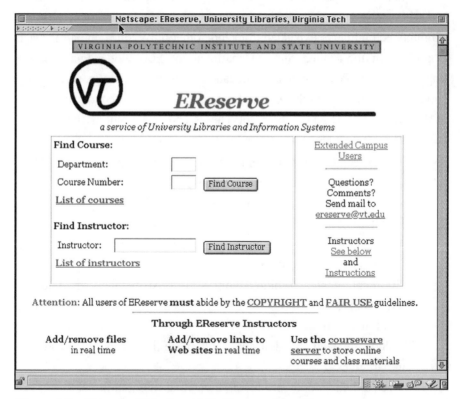

Figure 4.2   EReserve Web site at http://reserve.lib.vt.edu.

ELECTRONIC RESERVES

When Virginia Tech's University Libraries began to discuss expanding its Reserve Desk functions in the early nineties, SCP developed a system that enabled instructors to put their class materials online. The initial electronic reserve system mapped Reserve Desk practices to Web processes so that in the spring of 1995, faculty sent their digital course materials to the library to manage and make accessible to students (see Figure 4.2). One drawback was a time delay while library staff determined that files had been sent, verified which course and instructor should be linked together, and moved the files to the appropriate directory. Advantages to the system included typical library services: once the faculty had sent the files, they were relieved of having to deal with them or the students who needed the information. Improved library services included twenty-four hour access and programmatic backups so those files would always be accessible throughout the semester.

The next generation of the system also allowed faculty to manage their class materials on a library server or to link from EReserve to files on another server. By the fall 1998 semester, EReserve evolved links to the university's timetable and course descriptions, relieving faculty of the need to complete a Web form with this information. The third generation system also made it easier to link to files on any server of class materials. Faculty use the same personal identification (PID) and password that they use with the university's e-mail system to become immediately linked to the registrar's current list of classes. From their list of classes, faculty add and remove files or enter a URL to link their classes to existing Web sites. Students also have immediate access to the links and files.

Many improvements in EReserve are a direct result of SCP collaborating with units outside the library. SCP oversees EReserve, while the computer storing the class information is under the purview of the registrar. The programs and scripts, along with the faculty database and their files, reside on another computer. The campus network links them all to EReserve.

The library oversees compliance with copyright law and fair use guidelines in the electronic reserve system so that access continues to be limited to our university community. Whenever access must be restricted, as with EReserve and some ETDs, all registered students and university employees are recognized as valid users whether on campus or off, through name proxy servers or IP addresses. (See the "Copyright" section on page 53.)

Some of EReserve's innovations are a result of SCP joining a university-wide initiative to provide current as well as potential students with improved and efficient access to Virginia Tech's online and electronically enhanced courses. Called VTOnline (http://vto.vt.edu), the Web site presents links to all of the university's electronic learning opportunities and information services, online degree programs, short courses, extension activities, and public service initiatives. It also links existing and new network-centered teaching initiatives, ranging from course and program innovations to intellectual property policies, and assessment and evaluation practices.

Figure 4.3   News reports from the Scholarly Communications Project
(http://scholar.lib.vt.edu/NewsOnline/NewsOhp.html).

NEWS ONLINE

SCP has enhanced library resources and services by collaborating with publishers as well as with users outside the university. Working with Landmark Communications in 1994, SCP began providing access to regional news for the Blacksburg Electronic Village (BEV). In collaboration with regional news publishers, SCP developed procedures and wrote scripts that programmatically linked daily news reports to the Web. News resources evolved from tape downloads to automatic predawn file transfers and HTML markup. New challenges included dealing with cumbersome quality and quantity control for files received daily. As a result, we relegated the programmed reindexing that enabled word searching to the weekends when network traffic was lighter and response times better.

An early goal of "news online" was to provide same-day Web access to printed news. The newspapers' in-house procedures and outdated technology, as well as the publishers' fear of losing paid subscribers, combined to curtail our meeting this goal. SCP ceased doing news downloads early in 1997 but still continues to provide historical reports about the region and the state (http://scholar.lib.vt.edu/VA-news/VA-news.html).

Through "news online," SCP accumulated valuable experience, including managing daily updates on the Web, implementing effective security precautions, and indexing large sets of files. SCP staff took this knowledge to a meeting with the station manager of the nearby CBS affiliate, WDBJ-7, who agreed that SCP would create a Web site from electronically transferred daily televised news files. SCP's programmer adapted the scripts and programmed procedures from newspapers to television news files. Since March 1995, news reports have been available within twenty-four hours of broadcast at http://scholar.lib.vt.edu/NewsOnline/NewsOhp.html (see Figure 4.3). Such timely availability is due in large part to the television news already being available in digital format from the closed-captions prepared for hearing-impaired viewers.

The opportunity to expand online news resources came again in March 1997 when NewsExpress, a Washington, D. C. newspaper distributor, invited SCP to participate along with four other libraries in an experiment to supply international newspapers online. The first newspaper, *Le Monde*, is available online in PDF format before it is available in paper on the streets of Paris or New York! *The European* from Great Britain came next and then *Ettella'at* (in Persian from Iran) and *Al Nahar* (in Arabic from Lebanon). About a year after this experiment began, NewsExpress was ready to terminate the free library access and offer paid subscribers continued access to *Le Monde* online. The library easily determined that this would be less expensive and would give greater access than maintaining current subscriptions to both the daily paper and periodic microfilm versions.

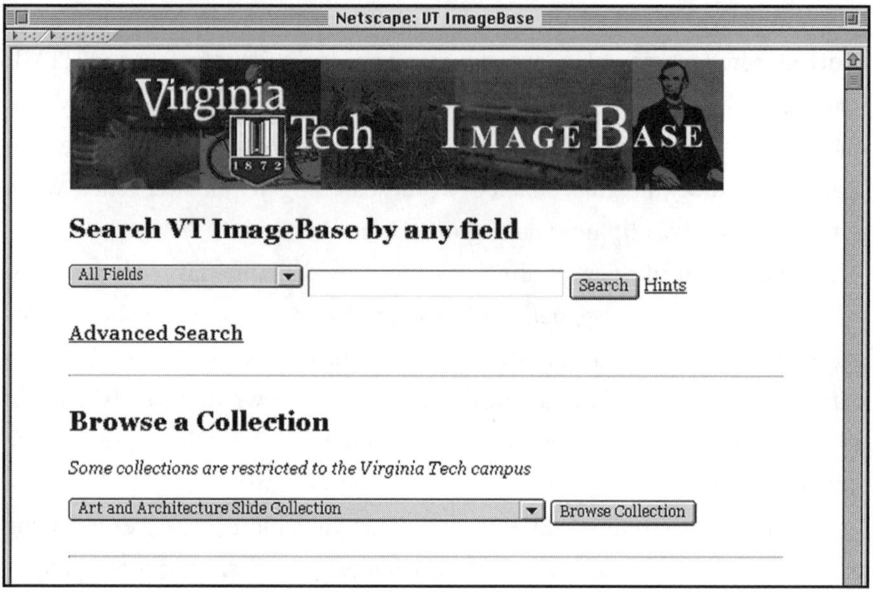

Figure 4.4   VT ImageBase at http://scholar.lib.vt.edu/imagbase/.

NETWORKED IMAGES

Digital image access was an obvious direction for SCP to turn next, but this is one area where we did not expect to receive original digital works. Digitizing, storing, identifying, and presenting non-textual files created new challenges. In 1994 SCP selected original watercolors of early cadet uniforms and fragile glass negatives from the library's Special Collections Department to initiate our online digital image collection. In the first generation of the digital image collection, SCP staff added brief text in Web pages and appropriate hypertext links.

The second generation added images extracted from a video laser disk originally prepared by a Virginia Tech architecture faculty member. Available staff rekeyed or scanned the index and linked the images to the index in typical Web fashion. Though unadvertised, SCP fields a growing number of requests for access to these images, especially by architecture students and history teachers. The copyright holder of the laser disk has not released the online images for use outside the university, however, so we cannot honor these requests.

The third generation was a major departure from previous systems. Named VT ImageBase, it was a searchable database of images and identifying information (metadata) that grew out of a small interdisciplinary working group that developed a tactical plan as part of the Information Systems' strategic plan (see Figure 4.4). The plan showed how, in the course of normal class preparation, faculty would select slides to be digitized, photographic experts would create high quality digital images, and the library would store and provide access to the images. This process would work as well for the entomology professor as for the art professor. Though the slides selected for the prototype had identifying information, this system enabled the faculty to elaborate on that information. ImageBase incorporated an early version of the Dublin Core metadata so that every image is associated with these standard element tags.

The working group envisioned many advantages to networked digital images over the typical analog slide collection used by most faculty. Instructors could display images in any order during a lecture and would no longer be tied to the order the slides were placed in the carousel. Students could view the images outside of class at any time—whether the slide library was open or not. With the success of this prototype, slide collections around the university could be systematically digitized for use in classroom lectures, and faculty and students would have access to all the digital images, not just the ones used in their classes. SCP staff followed through and constructed a prototype with 300 art history slides and related metadata which are now part of the VT ImageBase. These images were incorporated into an art history course which was taught fall semester 1996.

With access to relatively inexpensive student labor, SCP hired students who derived small "thumbnail" images and larger full-screen images from the "archival" TIFF images prepared by the experienced staff at PhotoGraphic Services (PGS). Next they entered the metadata, and linked the images and identifying data in the database. As they digitized images, PGS sent the TIFF to a Computer Center machine that is accessed by SCP students to create user-friendly image displays and later by PGS staff when reproductions are contracted and paid for through Special Collections. PGS later purchased Kodak CD equipment and software to prepare, store, and ship all digital images to Special Collections. We then modified our workflow accordingly.

Several challenges had to be addressed before this plan could be fully implemented. The major downfall was not with the prototype but with available classroom equipment. Not a single classroom on the Virginia Tech campus included the appropriate technology to display digital images with the same clarity—sharpness, distinct lines, and vibrant colors—now available to project 35mm slides. That students had online access to the images associated with each day's lecture, in addition to improving instructors' lecture contents and classroom environments, was not sufficient incentive (in the design team's opinion) to garner faculty participation in a large image conversion project. These challenges remain, but the fast campus network and construction of the Advanced Communication and Information Technology Center (ACITC), may combine to provide the necessary incentives for broader participation in the VT ImageBase.

Through financial support from VIVA, the Virtual Library of Virginia, the VT ImageBase grew steadily for two years. As of August 1998 there were over 14,000 unique and fully identified images. All descriptive elements are indexed and can be searched individually or in combination.

ACCESS: OPEN AND RESTRICTED

The library has a philosophy of open access. Virginia Tech is a state institution; therefore, its library is open to any citizen of the Commonwealth. Accordingly, the Scholarly Communications Project has encouraged all of its collaborators and contributors to provide unrestricted access to their works. We have met with varying degrees of success. Our ejournal editors have been willing to allow unrestricted access with the caveat that they could later change their access options. However, editors have not made any access option changes to date—all are available without restrictions (and none have lost paid subscribers, according to SCP ejournal editors informally polled). When access had to be restricted for other SCP resources, we negotiated university-wide availability as is the case with regional and international news, commercial ejournals (e.g., MIT Press and Birkhauser, Boston), and is an option available to ETD authors.

There was only one situation when SCP initiated limited access—mapping traditional Reserve Desk services to a comparable but enhanced Internet service. Virginia Tech EReserve adheres to copyright law in the same way that the library's Reserve Desk does. Just as the library provides materials from its Reserve Desk, members of the university community have access to digital materials that the faculty prepare and link to EReserve. Online access is more restricted in some ways, however, than the traditional Reserve Desk because faculty and students using EReserve are verified when they access the system. Validating a user's status is a fairly new concept, especially at state supported institutions like Virginia Tech that allow any citizen of the Commonwealth to use library collections.

Restricted access is monitored through two validation systems. The most commonly known system is usually referred to as "limiting by IP address." That is, the server with the library resources requested validates that the user's computer is registered with the university. If the Internet address of the computer is registered, access is permitted; if not, access is denied. Similarly, but through a somewhat more cumbersome process, university faculty, staff, and students who are away from campus computers can use the "proxy" functions that are components of Web browsers such as Netscape and Explorer. This function has users enter their personal identification (PID) and password as they are registered with the university. This system validates the user rather than the user's computer, but both require that the university maintain up-to-date registers of computer addresses and current university members' PIDs and passwords.

Today many of the library's online systems rely on these name servers to control access through user recognition systems. Our interlibrary loan and document delivery systems require online computer/user validation for requests entered online. The library has also contracted with many vendors for Web access to a variety of indexes and full-text databases. These contracts usually require that the library guarantee that only its students, faculty, and staff have access. Others not affiliated with the university have access when they are on campus and enter through the university's computer network, just as they might walk through the doors of the library and take a work off the shelf. These digital library components are already full services of the library.

COPYRIGHT

Libraries that offer evolving digital content and services are frequently called upon to add new services. One such role of the Scholarly Communications Project has been developing expertise relevant to online scholarship, and then coordinating and sharing the knowledge gained. The library has long been a guardian of copyright through thoughtful and law-abiding policies for interlibrary loans, reserve, photocopy services, and more. However, as Web sites proliferated, inconsistencies in policies developed and the library lost track of the reasoning behind policies. Therefore, SCP and selected User Services staff (including branch, reference, and Reserve Desk staff) met and evaluated policies, agreed upon common practices among service units, and developed a Web site (http://scholar.lib.vt.edu/copyright/) to share what had been learned. This site includes interpretations of copyright law, links to the text of the law, sample letters to request permission to use someone else's work, links to publishers' e-mail addresses, advice for authors about negotiating to retain some rights, as well as current library policies.

Because faculty, especially those expanding into the realm of distance education, asked an increasing number of questions about copyright, SCP began sharing its knowledge outside the library at the summer 1998 Faculty Development Institutes. Hour-long sessions began at the Virginia Tech copyright Web site; focused on the rights of creators/authors, a thorough review of fair use, and public domain issues; then concluded with library policies especially for teaching and learning through online course materials and EReserve.

ARCHIVING AND SECURITY

Other than time-sensitive class materials, a research library generally favors archiving indefinitely what it has accessioned. Therefore, when the SCP was initiating new works and aligning procedures for online resources with past practices handling hard copies, we seriously considered the thorny issues of archiving and security. Initially, many of our authors, editors, and collaborators felt uncomfortable knowing that there is not always a paper backup. However, having paper provides many with a false sense of security. Library staff are particularly aware that a book may be checked out, may not be returned, and may not be replaceable. When this happens, there usually is not a backup copy on hand for several reasons, including the added costs of processing, reshelving, and storage.

One of the most outstanding and beneficial attributes of digital library resources, in addition to twenty-four hour user access, is that the library is committed to security and archiving. We make frequent backups, storing them online and off-line, in the same room as the server and in other rooms and in other buildings. When equipment fails, replacements are available, and there are copies of the information resources that can restore any work that was lost. This is not the case with most library resources in nondigital formats. Programmed backups eliminate labor-intensive processes transferring them from one location to another. Backups are also not bulky and do not accumulate at rates that require the construction of new buildings to house an ever-growing collection, as is the case with books and journals. SCP drafted archiving policies specifically for ETDs, and these can be generalized to all of our online resources. (See http://scholar.lib.vt.edu/theses/archive.html.)

STAFFING

Archiving and providing access to ejournals, news, and theses, and designing and maintaining reserve systems and the image database are huge accomplishments for a very small unit of 1.5 FTE with less than $100,000 in operating expenses (including student wages but not staff salaries). In 1989, the Scholarly Communications Project began with two half-time positions; the Library Automation Department shared one of its programmers and Technical Services shared a serials librarian. In 1994 a half-time clerical assistant from Technical Services joined SCP to focus on HTML tagging for electronic journals, and the SCP director officially devoted full-time to the Scholarly Communications Project. The technical assistant's position was subsequently upgraded to full-time, in part because there was less need for data entry.

The gradual weaning of two positions from technical services is partial evidence of the changes technology has created within the library organization. Further evidence is the 1996 upgrade of the technical assistant's position to that of a programmer so that manual processing tasks could be completed programmatically through in-house scripting. The director, however, also began overseeing Special Collections in 1996. In mid-1998 the programmer reverted to Library Automation and the Technical Director (programmer/analyst and systems administrator) joined SCP full time. As additional staff time and positions became available to the SCP through redeployment of library resources, the quality and number of online resources and services also increased.

Though staff support has gradually increased, personnel resources are minimal considering the number of resources SCP stores, preserves, manages, and provides access to, and the systems it designs and maintains. On only three occasions has SCP solicited new projects—television news reports, EReserve, and ImageBase systems design. Many Virginia Tech faculty participate in scholarly journal editorial boards, but SCP does not seek to convert their journals to online access because of a fear of attracting more responsibilities than we can handle well. SCP was created initially to experiment in scholarly communications but not to put its prototypes into production or to maintain heavily used services. It struggled to maintain EReserve at a high level of service until the service could be shared more broadly with Information Systems where two previous SCP personnel are now employed. The success of ETDs tests the limits of SCP's resources. In the last few years the budget for this unit has not increased, but the number of faculty and students served and the size of the ETD collection has grown dramatically.

HARDWARE AND OPERATING SYSTEMS

All of SCP's resources and services existed for over six years on an Apple NeXt that had been purchased in 1990. Initially used as a Gopher server, it began operating also as a Web server in February 1993 and functioned very well until 1997. From 1995 to 1997, SCP expanded to three servers, splitting the large and rapidly expanding image and newspaper files from the files of scholarly electronic journals and ETDs. In October 1994 SCP resources measured 479Mb, up from the 78Mb of storage we were using in January 1994. In June 1995 SCP measured 4Gb of scholarly electronic works; most recent measurements show SCP at 15Gb.

In October 1997, the original server migrated from the NeXt to a Sun Netra with a 200 MHz Ultrasparc processor and 128 Mb of RAM. It now runs the Netscape Enterprise Server on Solaris 2.6 and Perl 5.004_01. To backup our system, we have a Sun 8mm Ultra Wide SCSI tape drive that takes 170m tapes with a compressed storage capacity of 40Gb. Our two older servers (a Dual-Pentium PC running Slackware Linux 3.0, and a Dec Alpha running Windows NT 4.0) now provide development space and backups.

The SCP's limited budget mandates that we do as much as possible with shareware from the Internet, in-house scripts and programs, and bargain prices. FreeWAIS served us very well until the funds became available in late 1996 to purchase the OpenText LiveLink search engine. Then we quickly learned to appreciate the faster searches resulting in more accurate hits, and users like the variety of display options available.

EVALUATION

The effectiveness of some of these services has been measured through student and faculty surveys. All students and faculty having class materials accessible through the Libraries' EReserve system were surveyed spring semester 1995. A majority of the students (75.4 percent) rated EReserve 1-3 on a scale of 1-5, with 1 being very easy to use. On the same scale, 83.3 percent of the faculty rated it 1-3. The same percentage of faculty had no trouble converting their files to the PDF, which was the required format, and 100 percent preferred EReserve to traditional Reserves. Increased use is another measure of satisfaction. During the spring semester of 1995 eight faculty made course materials available for ten classes. By the 1996 spring term, 31 faculty taught 39 classes using EReserve materials. One week into the 1998 fall semester, 99 faculty used EReserve in a total of 131 classes.

Ejournal access logs also show dramatic increases in users every year. Gopher access increased nearly 300 percent during 1993–1994. World Wide Web access to ejournals increased more than 1,100% during 1994–1995. Another indicator of the success of ejournals is in the growth of the number of ejournals available. The Scholarly Communications Project made five ejournals available in 1993–1994. As of August 1998 there were seventeen full-text ejournals out of fifteen current and five dead titles.

In both of these sample areas, EReserve and ejournals, the Libraries' services have changed over time to respond to user needs. For example, EReserve originally accepted only PDF files. Now all file formats are accepted, including links to Web sites outside the library and the university. Initially the library's EReserve server provided faculty with space for their course home pages, but now a powerful Information Systems server is used. It is available for faculty and other instructors to store online courses and supplemental class materials. In addition, the "courseware" server can also be used to mirror existing course sites, to provide searches for course materials stored on that server, to support class chats, and to restrict access to materials as needed. The limited staff resources accomplish more when faculty prepare e-course materials (including scanning articles) and determine how their materials will be presented, accessed, and archived.

CONCLUSION

The Scholarly Communications Project is an example of how libraries creatively use existing resources and evolving technologies to improve services and increase the wealth and the quality of information available to their user communities and more broadly to digital library users. Pilot projects in electronic archiving and access systems have become standard library resources and services in many academic libraries. On-campus and remote users have access to both open and restricted resources, improving patron services as well as broadening instructional activities. With faculty and student support and with collaboration with other units, the library has established a variety of new resources, access methods, and services that are available for remote and on-site users. Especially significant is the library's ability to develop new services as needed.

Without support from Scholarly Communications, university research and scholarship would be long delayed in reaching students and faculty through traditional publishing and library processing routines. Students, researchers, and scholars would not have constant access to the wealth of our university community's research and scholarship available in its electronic journals, course materials, and ETDs. Their use would be limited to the operating hours of the library or to availability when other patrons have not removed them from the shelves. The library of digital resources and services already exists and is constantly expanding within the University Libraries at Virginia Tech.

With additional support, the future of SCP could include outreach to faculty to better inform them about what assistance is available from the library and to promote current and new technology initiatives. SCP could also build on current strengths, such as promoting greater innovation in electronic journals and making the VT ImageBase more broadly applicable to the university. Further work needs to be done in a variety of areas, including intellectual property management, archiving and preservation, multilingual appeal, metadata, automatic generation of MARC, and keywords to controlled vocabulary. SCP should place greater emphasis on the evaluation of resources and services beyond log file analysis. But, the limitations of current staff and equipment make these difficult to accomplish.

SCP is one arm of an evolving academic library. By stretching existing resources, Virginia Tech has consciously melded a digital library into the expanded collections and services of the University Libraries. The benefits extend beyond the campus to the Blacksburg Electronic Village and to members of our university community, wherever they are around the world. Libraries are enhanced when they incorporate digital resources and online services. Digital libraries more fully serve the information needs of their user communities when they expand to provide access to resources and services in nondigital forms.

The Scholarly Communications Project at Virginia Tech's University Libraries has created a variety of partnerships with units and individuals within its university community to produce unique online resources particularly suited to digital library resources and services. Through activities like those at http://scholar.lib.vt. edu (see Figure 4.5), libraries demonstrate that they are vital—fulfilling their mission to provide current as well as historical works and expanding services to meet the needs of on-campus and extended learners and faculty.

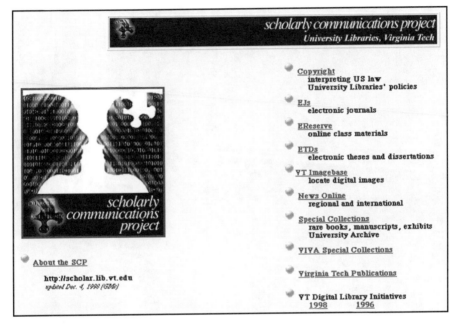

Figure 4.5

Library-Generated Databases

Tore Brattli
Academic Librarian
University Library of Tromsø
Tromsø, Norway

The development of the Internet and the World Wide Web has given libraries many new opportunities to disseminate organized information about internal and external collections to users. One of these possibilities is to make separate databases for information or services not sufficiently covered by the online public access catalog (OPAC) or other available databases. What's new is that librarians can now create and maintain these databases and make them user-friendly. Library-generated databases can be available to users at home and at the office. In addition, these databases can become powerful information services by linking to other databases, services, or information on the Internet.

This chapter will focus on the organization of information that can be done by librarians locally in each library. The emphasis is primarily on bibliographical references. As I examine why local organization is still important and why internal databases are the best tools for much of this work, you will also see how internal databases can be created and made accessible on the Web. In addition, several cases will be presented. The aim is to become aware of some of the useful things a local library can do with the new information tools that have arrived. The view is from an academic librarian at the University Library of Tromsø in northern Norway.

ORGANIZING INFORMATION IN LIBRARIES

These are the main tasks of academic libraries:
- Have collections of documents locally available

- Organize documents so that it is possible to be aware of and retrieve the relevant ones
- Educate and help users so that they can find the information they need
- Archive documents so that they do not get lost for the future

Traditionally, much of the organization of documents has been done locally. Librarians have systematically arranged local documents on the shelves, maintained a primary catalog, and created bibliographies and specialized catalogs for specific purposes. It's my impression, based on what I have observed in libraries with which I am familiar, that this work has been declining in recent years, and there are at least two reasons for this. More and more of the large-scale organization of references is done externally. For journal articles, this has been the main rule for a long time with indexing and abstracting services on paper, CD-ROMs, and online databases. For books, it has changed more recently with libraries sharing OPACs and downloading ready cataloged and indexed records from external sources. On the Internet, search engines and subject indexes are dominating, and most librarians have not entered this arena yet. Generally, it seems that the organization of references has shifted from local to national, and even to international.

The other reason is that it has been difficult to compete locally with the technology of large networked reference databases and OPACs, even if librarians were to have something interesting to offer. Users are not very keen on using paper bibliographies or catalogs anymore, and so far the tools for creating and publishing user-friendly databases have been too difficult for the average librarian to use. Large-scale organizing is efficient and gives access to large amounts of information, but unfortunately for many librarians, it has reduced much of the organizational responsibility to just routine registration.

The time has now come to turn this trend around. For libraries, the task of organizing information also means supplying different groups of users with tailor-made relevant bibliographies and special catalogs. As we will see later, it's impossible or at least very difficult for large external databases to take care of every need for information in each and every library. For libraries that want to offer a first class service, some organization still has to be done locally. With the Web, librarians finally have the information tools that make it easy to create powerful, user-friendly, accessible, and tailor-made databases that can be important supplements to the large reference databases and OPACs.

THE FUTURE

In the library of the future, the virtual (digital) networked library, there are strong indications that collection and archiving will be less important, at least in each local library. With networked information, there is less need to store local copies, and there is a shift away from collections and toward access. This might imply fewer libraries and less information in each library. Of course, other interesting opportunities exist for a library to collect documents. Some suggest that collecting and publishing local unpublished information may be an important future role of libraries (Webb, 1997). Others see the library as the publisher of local research material, bypassing today's publishers; however, this will not produce the same volume of documents as today. When libraries do not collect as much, there is less need for local archiving. The task of archiving will probably be assumed by regional and national archives or libraries in each country.

When it comes to organizing information and educating users, everything depends on the levels of motivation and skills available in the library for doing such tasks. One thing is quite sure: both tasks—organization and education—will become more important in the future. The amount of information is increasing very quickly, and users must be able to determine and locate relevant information for themselves. With smaller local collections, there will always be more limited organization of documents even though identification of their locations will be a part of the large-scale external organizational efforts. What is left is the task of serving our primary users with tailor-made information about documents relevant to their work. This important task will become even more crucial in the future. The tools for accomplishing this are databases with Web access. We must learn to create such databases and reaffirm our professional reputations for excellence at small-scale organization skills. In addition, contact with the users is important. If the users don't come to us, we have to visit them.

PUBLISHING LIBRARY-RELATED INFORMATION ON THE WEB

The World Wide Web is the most recent piece of a large technological puzzle, and it will revolutionize the library's opportunities to serve its users with information. Already many libraries offer a significant quantity of information on the Web. So far what is available is mostly information about information (i.e., metadata or references) and general information about the library and its collections. However, the revolution has just started. Digital journals are emerging in increasing numbers, and digital books are probably not that far behind. On the Web, information is published as Web documents (or pages). There are basically two different methods for generating Web documents, and both are equally appropriate for libraries to use. We may call them "static" and "dynamic" documents.

STATIC VS. DYNAMIC WEB DOCUMENTS

A static Web document is what most Web users would regard as the "normal" Web document. It consists of text, graphics, and HTML code—all stored as ready-to-use files on the Web server. When a user requests a static document, the files are sent to the user's Web browser and displayed. Static documents are normally best suited to information which is not easily listed and which does not change very often. Typical information to publish as static documents would be general library guidelines, information about the collection, hours of operation, user education, and lending/borrowing rules. Of course, full-text documents are static documents as well.

Dynamic documents are the opposite of static documents. These can be generated on the fly in response to a request from a Web user. Generally this means that dynamic Web documents did not exist before being requested. Dynamic documents are often the result of a database search, made by a computer program, based on a data file and a search string. Such dynamic documents are what I envision as the appropriate format best suited to publish local library databases.

EXTERNAL VS. INTERNAL DATABASES

Library databases can also be divided into external and internal (or local) databases. The distinction between the two concepts is not always quite clear, and what seems external to one person may seem internal to another. It actually depends more on the user's purposes than on the intrinsic structure or information in the database.

External Databases

External databases are databases that are externally operated in a way that the local library or librarians have little influence on content or functionality. Typical external databases (independent of medium or location) are the large reference databases for journal articles like Medline or Science Citation Index. OPACs are often regarded as external databases, but this of course depends on the actual solution. For libraries collaborating with other libraries about the OPAC or for libraries using commercial OPAC systems, this may often be the case. External databases—whether specific by program or content—are often more library independent than internal databases.

BIBSYS (http://www.bibsys.no/), the Norwegian national OPAC for universities and colleges, was actually one of the first in the world available on the Web (in November 1993). Since then, many other OPACs and larger reference databases have become available on the Web. Many libraries have developed reference databases that are integrated with their OPACs for holdings and online article ordering. Linking to full-text articles has also begun. Together with static documents these Web services can offer users nearly all the information they need about the local library and its collections, in addition to information about books and journals in general.

Internal Databases

Most libraries have so far been publishing information as static Web documents and as elements of external databases. In addition, practice often shows that there is a need for a third format: library-generated or internal databases. Internal databases are databases made within the library in a way that the library has more control over content and functionality. Typical internal databases may be catalogs of the library's journals or video collections, or bibliographies of famous local authors. Internal databases are often more library dependent or more tailored to a specific group than are external databases. They are better suited to cover local specialties. For most libraries, internal databases will be an important supplement to external databases. Yet, as a tool, internal databases for the library are a bit like bibliographic management software such as ProCite or Reference Manager for scientists.

What Is Special About Internal Databases Now?

Of course, internal databases are not new (Biggs, 1995; Brudvig, 1991; Raeder, 1989; Smith-Cohen, 1993). Librarians are trained to realize that objects can be described in terms of their structural commonalities. The best way to organize these objects is to make bibliographies or catalogs (i.e., "databases") of the descriptions. Therefore librarians have made lists, i.e., bibliographies and catalogs for books, journals, and articles, and then made these lists available for users. This has always been one of the more important tasks for librarians, and still is.

With the introduction of computers, however, it seems that librarians have been inhibited, or at least limited, from taking part in the latest bibliography and catalog developments by difficult-to-use-technology. This has been especially noticeable in the cases of smaller or tailor-made applications, requiring help from computer experts. The news now is that along with the Web there have arrived information tools which make it fairly easy for librarians to create internal databases and for users to access them. The databases can be made more user-friendly and, together with the possibilities for integration with other information, can increase the chances that the new databases are really used. Of the four improvements mentioned, the design and use functions have been more evolutionary while the database access and integration through the Web have been truly revolutionary.

Easy to Create, to Access, and to Use

We no longer need to be computer experts to create user-friendly Internet-accessible databases. With minimal training most librarians can now create and maintain relatively advanced Web databases. This allows them to focus more on content than technology and to create databases for particular purposes. This is especially important for smaller libraries and even for librarians in larger libraries who do not have access to support from computer consultants or management. The creativity can finally grow again!

With the worldwide Internet, it is easy to make the databases accessible wherever the users are, whether at home or at the office, and twenty-four hours a day. The databases are now user-friendly in every way—in the installation of search software, in the searching, and in the presentation of information.

INTEGRATION WITH OTHER INFORMATION AND SERVICES

Last but not least, internal databases can function as powerful information services by integrating them with information and/or services on the Internet. Records in an internal database can easily be linked to records, searches, or services in other databases or to external information or full-text documents on the Internet.

At the local level, an internal book database entry for a specific title may be linked to its associated records in the OPAC, or to the publisher's page about the book. This gives the user bibliographic information, location, loan status, loan order, table of contents, and description of the book. In a database of journal entries, titles can be linked to the OPAC for bibliographic information and article ordering, to the publisher's pages for table of contents, or to related reference databases. A locally generated Shakespeare bibliography can be linked to external full-text materials and to other information on the Web. A thesaurus or a classification table (databases of classes or subject words) can be linked to subject searching in reference databases and can be an alternative search interface to both internal and external databases.

ADAPTABILITY IS ESSENTIAL

In many cases the databases that are desired locally would have been best realized as an available OPAC function. The information is often already within the system, but it is not possible to access or present. The problem is often a lack of functionality in OPAC software along with too little interest or financial incentive to improve it. An example of this in the case of BIBSYS, our Norwegian national OPAC for universities and colleges, is the system's inability to search and present a list of recently purchased books. All the necessary information is present but it is not searchable. Instead, more and more local libraries must spend time and effort making their own internal databases in order to obtain this frequently required information. For instance, we wanted from BIBSYS a sorted subject list of our library's journals. Yet this need was not met, if indeed it was even recognized as a legitimate need.

The solution, of course, is that external databases should be made more flexible when it comes to searching for and presenting information. Still, it is not possible for an external database to cover every need in every library.

One problem with large databases is that they cannot do everything wanted (Spore, 1991; Gates, 1989). In order to satisfy many users and libraries, they often end up as the lowest common denominator of all needs. Only the most basic functionality and information fields are offered. Even if they contain many records, there are often limitations in searching, presentation, and information that each record contains. The result is disarranged quantities of valuable information that cannot be suitably extracted.

Some of the problems with large databases are as follows:

- High flexibility in searching, sorting, and presentation demands many indexes which in turn are processing and storage intensive.
- Functionality and data structure is difficult to change because of the size.
- Many options can actually be user-unfriendly (at least for the average user).
- Large databases tend to both hide relevant documents and to retrieve many irrelevant documents, especially for subject searching.
- It's not possible to reflect all the different aspects of each document in one database.

Because of the needs and problems mentioned, it is not possible, practical, or economical to satisfy every need in one database. In addition, large databases are often externally controlled and operated. Experience often shows that this makes it difficult even to convince the database producer that your library or users actually have a "need" at all. The adaptation of external databases to local needs is difficult because the databases often are large, complex, and externally managed.

COMPENSATE FOR LIMITATIONS
IN OTHER ACCESSIBLE DATABASES

The main reason for the library to want to build its own internal databases is to compensate for limitations or defects in other accessible databases. For example, suppose it was simple and flexibly easy to download information from external databases into internal databases. This would better take care of local needs. With powerful PCs and fast networks, even regular downloading of whole portions of the OPAC should be a possible option. An example of such a large scale downloading is the Computer Science Library at the University of Oslo, which every week receives a copy of all of its records in BIBSYS in order to update its internal database (Hegna, 1994).

Another compensatory local adaptation which we can all appreciate is the management of references. The best tools to make collections available are databases. Static Web documents are more suited to general textual descriptions. For references, the work of creating and updating presentations is demanding, and searching must be limited. The users are not a homogeneous group, and the need for information will vary with different groups of users. The challenge for the library is to make all kinds of collection options available for all different groups of users. Again, adaptability is essential.

The best tool to register, organize, update, and disseminate detailed information about a collection is a reference database. In a reference database the documents are represented by surrogates (references) which only contain key information about content and location, and therefore take little space. This makes it feasible to create databases covering most documents published in a subject area or contained in libraries. Reference databases make it easier to become aware of relevant documents without having to read all of them. This is, of course, especially important for external documents. With the Web, references are becoming increasingly more important because of the possibility of making links to the documents they are representing, wherever they may be. Most academic libraries today are fairly well equipped with reference databases for journal articles and an OPAC which includes books and journals.

The most cost-effective way to create reference databases is to make them large in terms of the number of records, and they should have a general functionality. This makes them useful for many users, and many libraries can share the work and/or operational cost. Examples of this are large reference databases like Medline, or OPACs like BIBSYS. These databases are important and powerful tools to extract relevant documents from the enormous amount of irrelevant material at a fairly inexpensive price. We can divide the limitations of external standardized databases into (1) information not possible to include, (2) selections of records not possible to search for, or (3) information not possible to present as desired. These three categories are not quite independent of each other.

INFORMATION NOT POSSIBLE TO INCLUDE

There may not be a commercially available or free database that already includes the particular information that is desirable for local needs. Though most established databases contain records and fields developed according to standard criteria, this also means that there are references to documents and information about documents that are not useful at the local level, although they meet the criteria. Two examples from BIBSYS that I have found involve searches of Web documents (records) and abstracts (fields).

INFORMATION NOT POSSIBLE TO SEARCH FOR

Generally speaking, when you are searching, the database returns the selection of records containing the information specified in the search string. If this information is not included, indexed, or possible to combine with searches in other indexes, you might well have an unsuccessful search. An example for me from BIBSYS is my attempt to limit the search to new journal issues received last week. Even though the date information is present and searchable, it may be difficult to make the database return the relevant selection of records exactly. For other instances of subject searching this is often the case, as well.

INFORMATION NOT PRESENTED WELL ENOUGH

Many databases offer very limited ways to present the retrieved selection of records. What is needed is a report generator, like those provided in most modern PC-database programs, where the user has nearly unlimited options and can:

- Choose which information to present from each record (fields, parts of fields or combinations of fields).
- Create layouts where the fields can be placed.
- Supply headings and extra text.
- Control typography.
- Control sorting.
- Send output to screen, printer or disk.

Most external reference databases unfortunately offer just a few of these features. If the limitations are serious enough, and there is no simple way to solve them, the solution may be to create internal databases to improve the situation. If you do not get what you want, you can now more easily make it yourself! Together, static Web documents, external databases, and internal databases will complement each other so that the library can offer a complete information service on the Web.

ADVANTAGES WITH INTERNAL DATABASES

I have attempted to demonstrate that one of the advantages of internal databases is the opportunity to serve specific users, groups of users, other librarians, and yourself. The needs of every science project or class with tailor-made expectations can be met with detailed information and functionality. This means that if there is a need for an alphabetical list of the library's journals and specific issue holdings, you can search out just that. With internal databases, it is possible to have more control of information, searching, and presentation. The use may be simpler, the noise (irrelevant information) lower, and the benefits higher.

Internal databases are also useful for promotion of specialties that often disappear in large databases. If your library has some interesting old books or some new and "hot" titles, it is difficult (and not acceptable) to tag them in the OPAC as "old and interesting" or "new and hot." With an internal database containing only old and interesting books, this is no problem. This is one of the reasons why many scientists have their own personal reference databases.

Each year libraries spend a lot of money on literature, but too much of this is seldom or never used because it had a tendency to disappear into the larger library collection. Through special promotion of different aspects of this literature—like famous authors, interesting newcomers, classics, or subjects of current interest—there is a great chance of increased use of such material. Such promotion is well documented for displays in the library (Baker & Lancaster, 1991), and perhaps it should be as effective using the Internet.

Also, collections other than books or journals can be organized with the help of databases. For some collections internal databases are the only option. Consider these possibilities:

- A database of pre-formulated searches for literature relevant to the most popular term-paper subjects in a primary course. For example, each search can be linked to the OPAC by subject, which then would always provide updated lists of books. This may save time and effort both for students and librarians.

• A database of (UDC, LC or Dewey) classes and descriptors linked to classification searches of the OPAC. This may offer an alternative search interface and access to something that users usually find difficult to work with.
• A database of FAQs (Frequently Asked Questions) about the library and services for users who want to learn about the library.

BENEFITS FOR LIBRARIANS

In addition to making collections available for the users, internal databases are great tools for academic librarians to manage their collections when the OPAC does not support this sufficiently. In fact, for several of the internal databases made at the University library of Tromsø, we feel that this collection support is reason enough for developing annotated databases. The extra added fields for comments, markings, prices, dates, use, etc., can be searched and presented in nearly any way needed to make informed decisions. Of course, much of this information can be downloaded each time from the OPAC and reformatted with a word processor to make the desired lists, but often such processing is more labor intensive than creating and updating a duplicate database.

Each year, an academic librarian at our library may purchase about a thousand books and subscribe to some five hundred journals. Because of large variations in ordering time for books, journal prices, currency, budget and feedback from the accounts department, the task of managing the budget can be a real challenge. Our internal databases for journals (with prices) and acquisitions of books (with order dates) are of great help in this work.

For collection development, internal databases can be used to divide acquisitions as fairly and professionally as possible among the different subjects and scientists. For books, we can more easily check how many are purchased in each subject. For journals, the database can produce user-friendly lists (sorted alphabetically, by price, or by subject) in order to evaluate the start of new and cancellation of existing subscriptions. With these lists, it is also easier to take advice from the scientists. The database can also prove important for operations like binding and discarding. The main advantage for journals is that a database can be used as a searchable notepad for assessments where the decisions often take much time.

A side effect of having internal databases is that the data can easily be examined or used for library statistics. It is also possible to register more information about each object than the main purpose of the database demands in order to derive more interesting results. Many OPACs have surprisingly few and limited statistical features. Examples of "research" information available from our databases are journal prices, book processing time, use, and the effect of library displays.

INTERNAL DATABASES AS AN INFORMATION TOOL

More and more reference sources and documents are now available in digital form on the Internet. This is most noticeable for bibliographic reference databases, but journal access is now increasing as well. We already see online reference databases linked to online journals. For books it is more difficult to tell because most people have an affection for books in their traditional form. As I see it, the success of digital books is highly dependent on screen technology. With cheaper, lightweight flat screens which are readable like books and use battery and mobile communication, much may change. It is likely that the number of digital books will increase in the future.

Another aspect of this situation is that much information is bypassing the library on the way to the users. For the library an important question is how this information should now be organized when it may never be present in the library. Databases should play an important role in this organization. Reference databases will be the main tool for organizing information about documents, in addition to becoming the virtual "bookshelves" for the same documents. Where the documents are located physically is of less importance as long as they are accessible. Large external databases will act as the general collections and internal databases as the tailor-made or special collections. The key to virtual libraries are reference databases (Morgan, 1998) and access to documents. This should imply that creating databases will be a substantial task for the librarian of the future. It is therefore important to learn the skills needed to organize information with the new information tools that have arrived. One way of doing that is to start creating internal databases.

HOW TO CREATE INTERNAL DATABASES

For librarians with a little interest in the Internet, there are several ways to create and publish their own internal databases. In this chapter a database is defined as a collection of related data, together with tools that can retrieve them effectively. It is important to choose the right tools and techniques to solve the problem. Simple solutions that many computer experts would call nonprofessional may still be the best. There is nothing wrong with that! There are big differences between large OPACs or other reference databases, and most of the internal databases that are useful to libraries. The former may consist of more than a million extensive records, while the latter range from a hundred to ten thousand brief records. These differences have major implications. Smaller databases do not necessarily need indexes, advanced relational structures, complex record formats like MARC, or large thesauri to do what they are supposed to do. Searching can be done sequentially, and there is no need to worry about storage capacity or redundancy of information. Even search fields are not necessarily needed. User-friendly searching can be done effectively by choosing (browsing) from menus with preformulated searches, instead of using search fields with more or less complex search languages.

CONTENT AND STRUCTURE

The first decision is which information to include in the database and how to structure it. This depends on the desired functionality and the possibilities for utilizing external information. Quantities of highly structured information allow greater search options at the cost of more updating and higher computer capacity. The easiest way to include information (at least virtually) is to link the database to external sources. This reduces the work of creating and updating the information to a simple update of its address. However, it is also necessary to have some information locally. The database must at least contain the information needed for local searching, sorting, presentation, and linking. A basic but sufficiently operational internal database may contain as little as a title, subject, and a link field.

LINKING

There are three different ways of linking internal databases to external information. First, we might link to static Web documents, database records, and database searches. The last two, of course, are basically the same (i.e., links to searches). A link consists of a link text, a link address (URL), and some HTML formatting code. All three must be included if the database is going to be able to produce a Web document with a real link. It is only necessary to store the variable part of the link text and URL in each record. The rest can be stored as a global constant. From this, the database can generate the complete link by merging the variable and the constant. Sometimes the variable is already included (e.g., title linked to OPAC records using ISBN); otherwise, it can be included in a separate (link) field. A second option is to link to Web documents by storing the complete URL. For records, it is often best to use unique identifiers like ISSN/ISBN or external record-ID. Links to searches give interesting opportunities and can be made from the actual search string or other already included fields. An example of the latter is to link each record of an internal journal database to search for articles in a reference database using ISSN. Unfortunately some information providers do not allow you to take this "backdoor" to their information (i.e., bookmark it). They want you to use their "main entrance," "shelves," and organization. This makes local adaptation difficult and reduces the availability of the information if your users will not be able to initiate fully the indirect route to the information on their own, using your path directions. Every library should demand the right to bookmark information they otherwise have access to, at least for purchased material.

LOADING AND UPDATING

In most cases, some of the information in internal databases will be a duplicate of information in OPACs or other reference databases. To avoid updating several places and/or to reduce the work, the best solution is to use a program that more or less automatically can extract information from external sources and update the internal database (Knudson et al., 1997).

One possibility is to use traditional downloading of a text-file which can be imported to the internal database. For a medium-sized library with modern PCs it is even possible to download the whole OPAC regularly (100,000 records at 2Kb; each is only 200Mb), if there is an option for this. Another way is the principle used by Web search engines, which regularly fetch Web documents (one at a time) from which they extract information. A more simple solution is to fetch records manually and copy (and paste) the relevant information, field by field, into the database. If the information is not available in digital form, typing or scanning may be the only solution.

In practice, a combination is often necessary. The degree of automation will usually depend on the possibilities to extract information from the original source, the possibilities to import this information into the internal database, the local programming skills, the size of the database, and last but not least, the rate of change in the information. There is no need for an advanced updating system for a small database with static information.

SEARCHING AND PRESENTATION

The advantage with smaller internal databases is that they can be presented in a Yahoo!-like way, using menus instead of, or in addition to, search fields. This is often simplest for subject searching. Using this principle, each Web document produced by the database is actually the result of a search and presents the list of hits (often titles) together with a list of other related preformulated searches. The searches should be chosen so that it is possible to retrieve each record, without the number of hits for each search being too high. For larger databases, this means many preformulated searches, which are then best organized in a hierarchical way. The clue is, of course, to index the records with the preformulated searches, which probably have turned into a thesaurus. In addition to menus, it is useful to have a search field. For quick lookup, the list of titles can be presented with holdings or call numbers. If more information is needed, the titles can be linked to local or external bibliographic information, full-text, more information from the publisher, etc.

PC DATABASES AND HTML FILES

As I have already stated, there are many ways to create internal databases. The solution depends on the size, functionality, computer skills, external help, financing, etc. One of the simplest ways to create and publish a database is to make a static Web document with indexes and a list of records, just like the good old bibliographic reference indexes or the phone book. Such a database has no search possibilities beyond the Web browser's "find in page" function, the indexes, or the order of the records. This is a perfectly satisfying solution for a smaller number of records, maybe up to a total of one thousand or a few hundred per Web document.

The best tool to administer, maintain, and format this kind of information is a PC database program. It provides user-friendliness and flexibility for the librarians operating the database. When some of the information is updated, the program can automatically find the right selection of records, sort them, format the right fields from each record with HTML code, supply adequate headers and footers, and export this to the Web server as ready-to-use Web documents (Delfino, 1996). This is the same principle used by producers of bibliographic reference books after the introduction of the computer, but now both the tools for making them and the medium for transmitting them are more effective and user friendly.

PC DATABASE, TEXT FILE, AND PERL SCRIPT

A more advanced solution is exporting the content of the PC database to the Web server as a presorted text file and using a CGI script to generate Web documents from this file. A typical text file format consists of records separated with paragraph marks and fields separated with the tab character. CGI scripts are small programs on the Web server (server extension programs), often programmed in Perl (Perl script), C or shell scripts, that users can start up and transmit information to. Perl is especially suitable because it is a high-level interpreted programming language with powerful abilities to search for and manipulate text. A Perl script can receive and interpret the search string, search the text file for matching records, format them with HTML-code, build a Web document, and return it to the user. Depending on the size of the records and the number of users, this kind of database works very well for up to 10,000 records. With a little programming skill, this is a relatively simple and flexible solution (Knudson et al., 1997; Zollman & Zollman, 1997).

PC DATABASE ON WEB SERVER

Maybe the best method, considering its simplicity, is to get a multi-user PC database program that can execute at the Web server. With a program like this, it is easy for us computer amateurs to create and maintain the database program, user interfaces, data structures, and automated routines. The information can be simultaneously updated by several librarians, and users can have direct and immediate access to the information. Several programs with these properties are available, and for some you can even define your own PC as the Web server. FileMaker Pro 4 (Langer, 1998) is an example of a general purpose, user-friendly PC database program which works very well for all the three methods mentioned so far. Recently, personal bibliographic management software like ProCite and Reference Manager (see http://www.risinc.com/) has arrived with options for database publishing on the Web. This will be of interest to librarians who want to create internal databases with Web access.

PROFESSIONAL SOLUTIONS

For large databases or projects with sufficient financial and technical resources it is possible, of course, to use more advanced database tools to develop more sophisticated databases. There are several possible ways to create these kinds of databases and to connect them to the World Wide Web (Lang & Chow, 1996; Ehmayer, Kappel, & Reich, 1997). The typical way to connect SQL databases, which are among the most common of professional databases, is by using a server extension program on the Web server. The program works as an interpreter between the Web browser and the database server. Extension programs can be homemade CGI scripts (Cox, 1998) or commercial products (Beiser, 1997; Perez, 1998) like Cold Fusion or HotSQL. The advantages of professional tools include greater flexibility and better performance for large quantities of data. The major disadvantage of professional solutions for the computer amateur, which most librarians are, is greater dependence on computer consultants. A more practical solution is simply to rely on external databases when your database goals become too complex. Other possibilities also exist. Internal databases can be hosted by commercial OPAC software (Morgan, 1998; Notess, 1993), or by utilizing programs for building Web indexes such as ROADS (see http://www.ilrt.bris.ac.uk/roads/).

TWO CASES FROM OUR LIBRARY

The University Library of Tromsø consists of two main libraries—one for science, medicine, and health, and the other for humanities, social studies, and law. In addition, we have some smaller scattered libraries serving a few of the off-campus institutes. The library for science, medicine, and health is the result of a centralization in 1991 when several institute libraries merged and moved into a new building. It is a typical research library with about 80 percent of the budget spent on journals.

Centralized libraries have both advantages and disadvantages. Before the centralization, the users from some of the institutes had to walk just a few meters indoors to visit the library and they did so nearly every day, if only to read the papers. They knew the librarians and the collections well, and they were aware of everything new and relevant that arrived. After the centralization this changed. They now have to walk several hundred meters outdoors to a much larger library with thirty librarians and large collections that are difficult to survey. Our location, Tromsø, is situated in the same latitude as Point Barrow, Alaska, and outdoor life can be a real endurance test, especially during the winter. We found that many users did not come to visit at all, and the rest visited the library infrequently and only when they had no alternative. Because of this, they missed many of the new books and journal issues that migrated into the large collections and thus these were rarely used. In both science and medicine, the latest books and articles are the most relevant because of the fast progress in research. At that time we did not offer any networked services, and everything was located in the library.

Something had to be done to change this situation. Moving or changing our new library was, of course, considered next to impossible. We had to give our users compelling reasons for visiting the library. We were not lacking in new and relevant books and journals—the problem was that the users did not know about them since they did not visit the library. Our solution was to reach out to them and give them some irresistible reasons to visit us. We decided to create a kind of virtual library that allowed them to easily check the latest week's new books and journal issues from their own offices. We hoped that if they discovered something interesting, and knew that they could go to the library and get it, they would do it.

THE JOURNAL DATABASE

We started work in 1993 by improving user awareness of our journals. We started with journals because we were mainly a journal library, and because the general situation for journals was unsatisfactory. At a minimum, our users needed answers to the following three questions:

- Which relevant journals does the library subscribe to?
- Does the library have this specific journal issue?
- Which relevant new journal issues have arrived lately?

The only information we could offer was the physical collection with 4,500 journals arranged alphabetically by title and an incomplete alphabetical list in the library with only the most basic bibliographic information. The situation improved in 1995 when journals were included in BIBSYS, but even today the functionality is far from adequate.

In June 1993 we created a FileMaker database through a combination of downloading and keying in records. This database could now print out complete and updated alphabetical and subject lists that we circulated among the scientists. Later, in June 1994, when we got our first Web server, the database could immediately export the same lists as Web documents and make them available on the Internet. In October 1994, we changed the list into a Web database using a Perl script and a text-file. The database (Brattli, 1998) has since been improved further with a Yahoo!-like interface (http://www.ub.uit.no/cgi-bin/tidsskriftdb/tid4.pl/T/Generell?lenke=lokal).

The core of the journal database includes four FileMaker databases, one for each of the participating academic librarians. Together they cover all the libraries' journals and all updates are done here. Each week the content from these databases is copied and merged into a complete journal database. From this database the content is copied to the Web server as a text file, and sometimes printed as a paper catalog available in the library. On the Web server, a Perl script generates Web documents from the text file dependent on requests from the users.

The four FileMaker databases are not similar but are tailor-made by each participating librarian. However, we have defined twenty-three common fields and formats because of the Web database and paper catalog. For these, each librarian has to supply data which includes local ID, title, holdings, location, subject word, classification, and subscription status. Other common fields include title change, ISSN, record ID in OPAC, content, latest issue, and external URLs. Fields only in FileMaker databases include price, budget, and comment fields for binding, cancellation, and discarding.

The Web database is built around a Yahoo!-like subject tree. For each subject an alphabetical list of journals with holdings is presented. The users can choose between titles linked to OPAC or local bibliographic information, including non-subscribed titles, and including titles from subordinated subjects. For some subjects it is also possible to choose a chronological list indicating the latest issues to arrive. Local bibliographic records give more information about each journal. They are in addition linked to the OPAC for article ordering and to the publisher for general information and table of contents.

With so many fields one would imagine that updating each database is labor intensive, but fortunately most information about journals seldom changes. The updating of new issues actually takes little time, maybe fifteen minutes a week.

RECENTLY PURCHASED BOOKS (NEW BOOKS)

The situation in 1993 was different for books than for journals. We had our excellent BIBSYS OPAC covering nearly all our books available in the library. The situation improved even more, especially for the users, from the end of 1993 when BIBSYS became openly available on the Web. Unfortunately for us and for the users, it was impossible to search for recently purchased books because the date fields are not indexed. Of course, we could search for year of publication, but that is not the same—for us it was important to be able to tell the users that certain books had arrived this week, others had arrived last week, etc.

Our new book database at http://www.ub.uit.no/cgi-bin/bok4.pl/B17/Informatikk?liste=utvidet&periode=92 (Brattli, 1997) is built on the same principles and has gone through the same stages as the journal database. So far, it only covers half of the library's subjects. Because of the large number of new books, we soon realized that it was best to keep the local bibliographic information to a minimum and instead link each title to its record in BIBSYS. For each subject the database presents a chronologically sorted list of titles of acquisitions over the last twelve months. The list is divided into three parts: books ready for lending, received but not ready, and books on order. The reason for including books long before they can be borrowed is that the users can make reservations at an early stage. This triggers rush processing, and the requester is notified when the book is ready. The linking to BIBSYS supplies bibliographic information, location, loan status, and possibilities for making reservations.

Updating is done up to three times for each book. When the book is ordered, title and record-ID (for linking) are manually copied from BIBSYS to the FileMaker database. In addition, subject is chosen from a menu (thesaurus) and the order date is generated. When the book arrives in the library, we just have to click on the record to generate the "date arrived" and the corresponding is done when the book is ready for loan, to generate the "ready for loan date."

With this database we have also kept statistics on processing time, use of books, and the importance of the new book display with respect to use.

BENEFITS AND USE

An interesting observation about these databases today is that the reasons for keeping them have changed. When they first were created, the main purpose was to inform the users about our books and journals. This is still an important use, but they have also become indispensable tools for us as academic librarians managing our collections. In fact, most of us feel that this is reason enough for keeping them. BIBSYS does not supply all of the data we need as the database is presently constructed.

We do not know whether the databases have led to an increase in the use of books and journals, but our impression is that they have. The importance is difficult to estimate, especially since so much has happened both with our OPAC as well as with the large external databases. We can envision our next research project to determine whether the internal databases lead to increases in use. At present we can only say that the use of the databases is satisfying to us. We need to publicize these services more to our users. Many users do not enter the Web at all, and thus we need to advertise the Web as well. Both for us and for our users, change takes time. So, did the databases solve our problems? The answer is, yes, some of them.

References

Baker, S. L. & Lancaster, F. (1991). *The measurement and evaluation of library services.* 2nd ed. Arlington, VA: Information Resources Press.

Beiser, K. (1997). Database-driven Web sites: Cold fusion for Web publishing. *Database, 20*(6), 48-50, 52.

Biggs, D. R. (Ed.) (1995). *ProCite in libraries: Applications in bibliographic database management.* Medford, NJ: Learned Information, Inc.

Brattli, T. (1997). Bruk av lokale databaser til informasjonsformidling og bibliotekforskning. *Norsk tidsskrift for bibliotekforskning, 10*, 51-74.

Brattli, T. (1998). Tidsskriftdatabasen ved Universitetsbiblioteket i Tromsø. *Ravnetrykk, 15.*

Brudvig, G. L. (1991). Tailoring a journal article database to local needs: Planning and management issues. *Journal of Library Administration, 15*(3/4), 85-100.

Cox, T. (1998). Using Perl with databases. *BYTE, 23*(5), 57-58.

Delfino, E. (1996). Automatic HTML-part 2: Creating HTML from a database program. *Online, 20*(6), 96-98.

Ehmayer, G., Kappel, G. & Reich, S. (1997). Connecting databases to the Web: A taxonomy of gateways. *Lecture Notes in Computer Science 1308*, 1-15.

Gates, R. (1989, October 17). Downloading info for local processing. PACS-L item 690. (PACS-L@LIST SERV.UH.EDU).

Hegna, K. (1994). Bidrag til idéen on det elektroniske bibliotek. *Bok og bibliotek, 61*(8), 25-30.

Knudson, F. L., Sprague, N. R., Chafe, D. A., Martinez, M. L. B., Brackbill, I. M., Musgrave, V. A., & Pratt, K. A. (1997). Creating electronic journal Web pages from OPAC records. *Issues in Science & Technology Librarianship 15.*

Lang, C. & Chow, J. (1996). *Database publishing on the Web & intranets.* Scottsdale, AZ: Coriolis Group Books.

Langer, M. (1998). *Database publishing with FileMaker Pro on the Web.* Berkeley, CA: Peachpit Press.

Morgan, E. (1998). We love databases! *Computers in Libraries, 18*(2), 38-39.

Notess, G. R. (1993, June). Offspring of OPACs: Local databases on the net. *Database, 16* (3), 108-10.

Perez, E. (1998). Supercharge your Web site: Cheap and easy Web-database apps! *Library Software Review, 17*(1), 24-30.

Raeder, A. & Tung, S. (1989). Downloading and converting bibliographic records from mainframe to micro using dBase. *Microcomputers for Information Management, 6*(1), 11-32.

Smith-Cohen, D. (1993). Developing an inhouse database from online sources. *Special Libraries, 84*(1), 9-17.

Spore. S. (1991). Downloading from the OPAC: The Innovative Interfaces environment. *Library Hi-Tech, 9*(2), 69-79.

Webb, T. D. & Zhang, B. (1997). Information dropshipping. *Library Hi-Tech, 15*(1/2), 145-149.

Zollman, K. & Zollman, D. (1997). Creating a simple searchable database on the Web. *Computers in Physics, 11.*

A Public Library in Transition:

Paradigm Shifts Toward the New Millennium

Don Napoli

Director
Saint Joseph County Public Library
South Bend, Indiana

PROFILE OF SJCPL

The St. Joseph County Public Library (SJCPL) serves 167,000 people in eight of the thirteen townships of St. Joseph County, Indiana, providing services to about 72 percent of the county population. It is the fourth largest public library in the state, with a main library located in downtown South Bend and seven branch libraries located throughout the city and other parts of the county. An additional 18,000 square-foot branch is now in the planning stage for a projected fall 1999 opening in a rapidly growing township. In its primary role as the "Information Services Hub for the Community," the St. Joseph Public Library became the first public library in the U.S., and only the second in the world, to run its own Web server and put up its own home page on the Internet (http://sjcpl.lib.in.us/). Since then, SJCPL's Web site has become one of the most bookmarked public libraries in the world, enjoying an average of over 12,000 hits per day. Much of this activity is due to the searchable Internet database SJCPL maintains with hypertext links to nearly 600 other public library home pages (http://www.sjcpl.lib.in.us/ Databases/PubLibServFind.html) throughout the world.

BECOMING AWARE OF THE INTERNET AND ITS POTENTIAL

The 1992 ALA Annual Conference in San Francisco was our initial introduction to the emerging role of the Internet within the library setting. When I had left SJCPL's main library in 1992 to attend the conference in San Francisco, my impression was that our then recent renovation and expansion project had made SJCPL a "state-of-the-art" facility. With its new computer workstations and its newly installed CD-ROM tower connected to those workstations throughout our main library, we felt we were ahead of most other public libraries. But then, at the conference, I passed by the Dynix (now Ameritech) exhibit and saw a Macintosh computer being used as an online catalog. Since our library staff and I were Macintosh afficionados, I was naturally attracted. The menu on the screen, however, was more than an online catalog. One of the selections was something called "The Internet." Selecting this by typing in the menu number brought me to a list of more choices, one of which was the National Library of Australia. I soon found myself searching for titles in the online catalog of a library that was over 7,000 miles from where I stood in San Francisco. I questioned the sales representative as to who was paying for this long-distance call from San Francisco to Sydney. How could Dynix afford to do this for everyone at the ALA exhibits? The answer was, "It's free—it's the Internet!"

Continuing through the exhibits, I came to the AT&T booth and a small exhibit called Minitel. I learned that Minitel, owned and operated by the French government, provides 17,000 information services, including everything from booking train and plane reservations to directory services and chat lines. Truckers could even find how best to move materials from one location to another. The French government had six million of these telephone devices in French homes logging over 1.6 billion transactions per year.

While at that ALA Conference I also noticed several "Internet" programs on the schedule, all of which seemed to be sponsored by academic associations with speakers from colleges and universities. Public library involvement was nowhere to be seen. I purchased some of the audiotapes at the end of the conference and listened to them in my spare time. One of them featured speaker Ted Nelson, who expounded on his concept of "nonsequential writing" or "hypertext"—a word he had coined over twenty years before. He described hypertext as a system for linking every published thought or idea to every other thought or idea to which it was related through electronic documents, with cross-references, backtracks, and alternate versions. This would create a complete system of knowledge interrelated and linked electronically through words that were connected to other documents and other words. He called these "hyperlinks." When I got back to South Bend, I discovered that the library had two copies of Nelson's most recent book, *Literary Machines* (1981). I consumed it, thoroughly absorbed by his vision.

We know now that just one year later (August 1993) Marc Andreessen and his team at the National Center for Supercomputing Applications (NCSA) at the University of Illinois, Urbana-Champaign, created Mosaic, the first Web browser. This revolutionary tool could implement Nelson's idea on a worldwide electronic network called the Web using something called "hypertext transfer protocol," or "HTTP."

SJCPL BEGINS INTERNET SERVICES

Back in South Bend, our public library entry into the world of the Internet was surprisingly straightforward. Pat Lawton, our main library's head of Adult Reference and Information Services, had read about the Internet and Minitel. Joyce Hug, our electronic database specialist, knew the university had access to the Internet because her husband was a physical chemist at the University of Notre Dame. Since our reference staff underspent the $10,000 budgeted to cover the costs of electronic reference searching on Dialog and similar electronic databases, we had funds available. I asked Pat and Joyce to find out from the people at Notre Dame how we might get on the Internet and asked them to use their budget for this project.

Through a computer class she was taking at the University of Notre Dame, Joyce Hug asked the instructor, Joel Cooper, assistant director of Networking Services at the University, how SJCPL might be able to get on the Internet. Joel put her in touch with CICNet in Ann Arbor, Michigan, a nonprofit organization that provided Internet services to the University of Notre Dame and to many other universities throughout Illinois, Michigan, Indiana, and Ohio. We started with a SLIP (Serial Line Internet Protocol) connection, a Macintosh (using a program called MacSLIP), and a 9,600 baud modem. CICNet provided us with the SLIP connection free of cost as part of a pilot project which was testing the SLIP software on Macintosh computers. Our only communication expenses were the long distance phone calls to a computer in Chicago that connected us to the Internet.

By September 1992 we were up and running. CICNet even provided us with an e-mail account on their server. We used such programs as Gopher, Veronica, telnet, ftp, and Eudora, all of which were free and readily available from such places as the gopher server at the University of Michigan. New versions of the developing software could be acquired by ftp practically every month.

DEDICATED 56K LINE

After almost a full year of using the Net and learning what sites had the best sources for answering certain types of reference questions, Joyce Hug informed me that we could link more than one computer to the Net at one time and also save on long-distance phone charges. To accomplish this, SJCPL needed to install a dedicated, leased 56K telephone line similar to what we used between our main library and our branches for our automated GEAC (formerly CLSI) circulation system.

The University of Notre Dame was willing to allow us to connect to their dedicated line out to the Internet. After looking at the costs and the proposed contracts with CICNet and Ameritech, our library board agreed, and by September 1993 we had a dedicated line on the Internet capable of handling many of the computers connected simultaneously to the new Ethernet network in our main library. We did not realize at the time that once we had established this type of dedicated connection to the Net, not only could each of our computers be a recipient or client for information from any other computer server in the world, but each one also could function as one of those servers of information worldwide. That paradigm shift would come a little later.

Convincing our library board to sign contracts with Ameritech and CICNet for undefined sources of information "out there" meant jumping through some hoops. A couple of board members were not enamored with how far and how fast we had come with our automation system and our increasing use of computers, and this was one giant step further in that direction. Providing a live demonstration at a board meeting did the trick. We found subjects on the Net that we knew would be of interest to certain board members. A rehearsal prior to the meeting helped smooth the way for our presentation and we were able to give the impression that we knew what we were doing.

The contracts were approved unanimously by the board with annual fees to CICNet totaling $4,500 (as our ISP) and to Ameritech totaling $1,880 for the dedicated 56K line. In addition, there was a one-time cost of $10,000 for router equipment and installation. We would save almost the entire cost of the annual contracts by eliminating just one CD-ROM subscription service with a for-profit reseller of government documents since we could now access this information over the Internet at a government Web site. Furthermore, it would be available on many more computer workstations without additional licensing fees. The economics of the Net were beginning to become evident to us even though this was only our first lesson.

With the 56K line installed, we were able to access the Internet from all our staff and reference computer workstations connected to our Ethernet network at the main library. Many more staff members were able to use telnet, Gopher, Veronica, ftp, and e-mail. The University of Notre Dame graciously provided SJCPL with ten e-mail accounts on its server so that even more of our staff could use e-mail.

PUBLIC ACCESS SERVICES

In August 1994 we dedicated two computers to public access to the Internet and became the first public library in Indiana to do so. Our seven branch libraries were given access through a dial-up connection to our Ethernet network at the main library. We used desktop Macs and 28,000 baud modems at each end (one at the branch and the other at the main library). Only five modems with five telephone lines, however, were installed at the main library for this Wide Area Network (WAN), and these were all connected to a Shiva NetModem. The five telephone lines were set up so that if one of the lines were busy at the main library, the call then cycled to the next available line and modem in the chain. Once connected to our WAN, branch reference staff gained access to our Internet router through our Ethernet lines and from there went out to the Internet. The assumption was that probably no more than five of our branches needed access at the same time, and there would be few busy signals. This assumption proved to be correct, even when we allowed two local high schools to use the same route of access and establish their own Web pages on our server. All of the computers using our WAN had to be Macintosh and had to use Apple Remote Access Client software with password access.

GOPHER AT THE REFERENCE DESK

In the fall of 1993, Pat Lawton, head of Main Library Reference and Information Services, encouraged me to work at the reference desk one Sunday. A user who came to me needed to see a copy of the new federal budget which had just been released the Friday before. Copies had not yet reached any of our libraries, but I was able to find an electronic version over the Internet on one of the federal government's gopher servers. I was impressed by how quickly any document, no matter what its size, could be made almost instantly available to hundreds of thousands of people. It took very little effort and involved practically no publication costs. In fact, the electronic version was better because now the digitized document was searchable electronically, could be copied and even transferred to other locations anywhere, and could be made accessible to many more people. The possibilities for the availability and flow of information seemed to grow exponentially overnight. We were now connected to everything that the federal government could put on their servers. We were becoming a federal government document center. A new age of access to documents and information more revolutionary than Gutenburg's printing press was in the making, and our library was part of the process.

SJCPL's COMMUNITY CONNECTION DATABASE AND PUBLIC ACCESS

Since late 1989, St. Joseph County Public Library has maintained several of its own home-grown, electronic databases. Our very first electronic database, created by Linda Broyles (now our Coordinator of Networking Services), was "Community Connection," containing detailed information on over 1,200 local community organizations and services. Community Connection was our local Information & Referral (I & R) file. The database was created with a very flexible and easy-to-use Macintosh program called FileMaker (now called FileMaker Pro). FileMaker allowed the user to create any number of fields of different types and sizes. It also indexed every field as soon as the information was entered so that every field was searchable. The program also allowed a user to search on any combination of fields using Boolean search strings. Its speed was very fast, returning any number of records within three seconds of starting a search, and it also had great sorting and report-generating capabilities.

Since we found FileMaker to be user-friendly and easy to understand, we now use it for all seven of our local databases. Staff member Dan Blacharski even published an article on our use of FileMaker (Blacharski, 1998). Our users can access and search these databases from our Web site over the Internet. Some have been up on the Web for over four years. Initially, however, we had not envisioned such far-reaching postings for our databases.

Several months prior to installing its 56K line (fall 1993), the library had been preparing to make "Community Connection" more accessible to the general public. We had planned to install it at a location near the main library's reference desk. We purchased two new Macintoshes for this purpose and attached them to a printer so that users could print their search results.

The day after the "Community Connection" press release appeared in the *South Bend Tribune*, Joel Cooper phoned to encourage us to install the database on Notre Dame's gopher server, which made it more generally accessible. He told us to convert the database to an ASCII text file (with certain changes) and deliver it to him on a floppy disk. When Joyce Hug and Linda Broyles delivered the disk to Joel at Notre Dame, he said he would have it loaded onto their gopher server and available on the Internet before they could travel the three-mile distance back to our main library. When they returned, they verified that it was indeed there and searchable over the Net. All of the reference computers that were connected to the Net could now use the database. In just the time it took to drive three miles, our "Community Connection" database was available from over twenty computers at our main library and to hundreds of thousands of computers worldwide at practically no additional cost to anyone.

Later that day, I asked Joel if the Notre Dame gopher server had any way to track how many times "Community Connection" was accessed over any given time period. Of course, it did! This was a capability that we did not have on the two Macintosh computers which we had just installed at the main library. When we called him a day later, he informed us that the database had been accessed two hundred times in the first twenty-four hour period. This was more than our reference librarians at the main library had accessed it in an entire week or more. Encouraged, I asked Joel if we could put up another of our FileMaker databases called TribIndex, an index of citations to newspaper articles dealing with local news in the *South Bend Tribune*. He balked a bit at first when I told him that the database was 8 megabytes in size, but then agreed. This too was made available on Notre Dame's gopher server. Prior to this, the TribIndex was available on only a few of our reference desk computers because of its size; now it was available on all of them connected to the Net. Our excitement about the potential of the Internet began to grow as we envisioned more possibilities.

MOSAIC INTRODUCED

In September 1993 Joyce Hug informed us that NCSA had just released working versions of its Mosaic program, the first Web browser, for all common platforms, including the Macintosh. Various sites had been using prerelease versions of Mosaic since June 1993, but it was not until October 1993 that I had a copy to use. New versions were being released practically every week, but the program was still clunky and crashed my computer every now and then.

I then started to look at NCSA's daily listing of new Web sites on its "What's New" Web page to see what new sites were coming onto the Net. I tracked what they were doing with this new protocol of hypertext, graphics, and sound—the multimedia expansion from what Ted Nelson had first envisioned. In addition, one of the most impressive developments Mosaic brought to the desktop computer was the integration of almost all of the previous Internet protocols, calling them up on the screen as "helper" applications as soon as one clicked on a link. Telnet, Gopher, and ftp could now all be accessed immediately from a hypertext document or Web page. This was very exciting stuff!

In February 1994, I noticed a new Web site called "The Orange Room" at the University of Notre Dame. The "What's New" blurb announced that the University of Notre Dame WWW server was now online at http://www.nd.edu. There was also an "underground" server, "The Orange Room," which was up and running from the university. Both had image and sounds, AppleScript-based services, and some great looking pages.

The "AppleScript" reference intrigued me. I connected to the Web site and read that the Web server was running on an Apple Macintosh computer and was being managed by a Webmaster named Mike Miller, a graduate student at the university. This "underground" Web site also provided Web pages

he students, an interesting concept that was new to me at the time. What
even more fascinating, however, was the fact it was not running on an
[or UNIX machine but on a Macintosh, and it was using AppleScript
ome of the tricks it did, such as an interactive visitor registration form!
sing Mike Miller's e-mail address at the bottom of the Orange Room
page, I wrote to him and told him about the new Apple Macintosh
dra 950 which our library had just installed in the administrative offices.
was one of Apple's most powerful network servers and at the time we
using it for the administrative office staff to share various files, such as
ry board agenda items, the budget, library policies, etc. In actuality, it
not being used much at all for all the power it had. I asked him if it
could be used as an Internet Web server. "Of course it could," he responded, and asked when we could get together.

SJCPL's First Web Server and Home Page

Mike Miller and I met with my library's Computer Room staff. It was at
7:30 a.m., March 14, 1994, in my office. Attending the meeting were Linda
Broyles, our Community Connection specialist; Joyce Hug, our Internet
specialist; and David Haslett, head of our Computer Room. I am so specific about this meeting because, at least for me, it was perhaps the most pivotal in terms of what we learned about the Internet. What Mike Miller
demonstrated for us in less than one hour completely changed our view of
the future and much of what we would do for the next four years. We discovered, with his help, that it was easy to publish documents on the World
Wide Web. In fact, it was frighteningly easy. This was a paradigm shift of
major proportions.

At that meeting we discussed the philosophy of publishing on the Web,
and Mike was ready for action. He started to fidget, shuffling in his hands a
couple of floppy disks that he had brought with him. He was ready to load
the content of those disks onto our Quadra 950. They contained the programs and files that we would need to get the Quadra started as a Web server. I invited him to the nearby room where the Quadra was located. Within
five minutes Mike announced that he had us up on the Web with our own
home page. He gave us the new URL (http://192.219.111.2), and we rushed
to the Macintosh computer in my office to access it using the Mosaic Web
browser. The first St. Joseph County Public Library's home page appeared

on the screen with a blue GIF image banner at the top saying "St. Joseph County Public Library, South Bend, Indiana," a brief "Welcome to the St. Joseph County Public Library home page!" in the middle, and a blue banner bar at the bottom of the page.

Mike explained that he had installed a new Web server program that he used on his "Orange Room" Macintosh called MacHTTP, created by Chuck Shotton, assistant director of Academic Computing at the University of Texas in Houston. Free copies of the program and its upgrades could be downloaded from the URL address Mike provided to us. He also gave us the disks he brought with him which contained the MacHTTP program, plus some other programs for making the creation of HTML documents easy— programs such as BBEdit. MacHTTP later became WebSTAR which is now sold by StarNine Technologies, Inc., located in Berkeley, California. It has become the most popular Web server software for the Macintosh.

Mike also mentioned a new MacHTTP listserv where one could follow the development of the software and learn tips on how to use it. New list-servs later grew out of this MacHTTP listserv, such as WebSTAR-Talk and WebSTAR-Dev. Other listservs dealing with supporting software also became very active, such as NetForms Talk, Netcloak-Talk, and FileMaker Pro Talk. These online discussion groups helped develop the software creators into large successful companies. Library listservs such as Web4Lib and PubLib also emerged during this period.

During those early years we learned the advantages of listservs: the rapid development of software through instant, worldwide collaboration, quick updates and widespread testing in different environments and on different platforms. We were able to share experiences with other librarians as we prepared to write specifications for a new automated system, and were even able to test those other systems through telnet sessions to their online catalogs.

We also learned that, as a public library cybercasting Web pages on the Net, we were alone! University library home pages were prolific, but after querying all the known library listservs which were then available, we could find only one other public library in the world with its own Web page—the City Library of Helsinki, Finland. Although a bit disappointed when we learned that they published their first Web page just two weeks before us, we were consoled when we realized that we were the first in the United States. We corresponded and collaborated with the Helsinki staff as we both developed and speculated about the future on the Web. Two years later (February 7–15, 1996), I was invited by the Finnish Library Association (Suomen Kirjastoseura) and the Finnish Ministry of Education to give five talks at two Finnish Universities (Tampere and Oulu) and at three of their largest public libraries (Helsinki, Tampere, and Oulu) about our SJCPL Web Server and home page. With a new laptop (Macintosh Duo 2300c) in hand and a digital camera, I traveled to the Arctic Circle and sent back news and images of the events. I was using a software package called Timbuktu to add images to our Web server remotely (http://sjcpl.lib.in.us/Finland/FinlandTrip.html). This let me share the experiences with my staff as I traveled. I asked myself, what would this new technology mean for the news or travel industries as they became more aware of the Net?

In November 1994 we created our Public Library Internet Servers List with links to the only five public libraries that we could find on the Web. Since then our list of hypertext links has grown to over 500 public libraries (http://sjcpl.lib.in.us/homepage/PublicLibraries/PublicLibrary Servers.HTML).

At that significant meeting on March 14, 1994, Mike Miller also showed us that the installation of a Web server was easy and fast. What was even more remarkable was that publishing anything on a worldwide basis was also quick and easy. The publishing industry was about to go through a revolution of major proportions! At the end of the Middle Ages the printing press replaced the professor's notes. All students could then have access not only to their professor's knowledge but also to the collective knowledge of many other professors on the same subject. With the Internet, anyone anywhere in the world could now publish without even going through the rigors of the publishing industry and peer review. This was a frightening shift for any librarian. How could one validate the authenticity and accuracy of any publication? What did this mean for libraries and librarianship? At the time I was too excited to worry about these thoughts as I started thinking about the possibilities of how our library might use this new medium.

After everyone left my office that day, I went to my desktop computer to look up the HTML standards and codes for what was being published on the Web. Accessing our new Web server remotely, I started to experiment with the HTML code and found that I could, for example, create a hypertext link from our new home page to the two searchable databases Joel Cooper had mounted on the Notre Dame gopher server. Looking at examples of how other Web sites constructed the code made it easy. In many ways it seemed as easy as the early forms of word processing. All one had to do was use the proper codes. In fact, many of the codes reminded me of what I had used in those first word processing software programs. I shared my excitement with Joyce Hug about how our databases were now available from our first Web page. We found that we could also create an introduction to these databases, to explain to the user what they contained and how they could be accessed. We could create other HTML pages for each of our departments at our main library and for each of our branch libraries, with links from the home page to each of them. We could provide a listing of our library programs, with links to the branches where those programs would be held. The possibilities started to grow as Joyce Hug and I started to learn everything we could about hypertext markup language. Since then, programs like Adobe Pagemill and Cyberstudio have rendered learning HTML codes unnecessary.

Soon after this meeting, we began purchasing a number of hardware and software tools that we needed to create Web pages. A color scanner (LaCie Silverscanner II) and a digital camera (Apple QuickTake 100) came first. A little later we added a data projector (Proxima Desktop Projector) to demonstrate the Web to others, especially to our staff. Software packages such as Photoshop were used to create and enhance GIF images, the graphic format that was prevalent at that time for transferring images over the Internet. As time went on, the ease and speed by which one could take a digital photograph of a library program or scan high quality photographs of a library building or department and place it up on a Web page for everyone to see became intoxicating. We invited each department and branch to submit text and photos for their own home pages and encouraged some competition for the best examples of what could be done. We learned how to create interactive forms and forums. We developed common gateway interfaces (CGIs), small programs that allowed our Web server to interact with other types of software programs, in order to create clickable maps. A map of South Bend and the locations of our branches came next, linking their locations on the map to their home pages. One CGI even provided a means to query our FileMaker databases through a Web browser (the first software package to do this was TR-WWW.cgi by Chris Priestley, followed by ROFM.cgi by Russell Owen) and send the search results back over the Internet through our server as an HTML document. Most of these early programs were experimental and free or shareware, but they kept opening up more exciting possibilities as Web pages started to become multimedia tools for publication and portals of entry to databases.

Management software such as WebStat (1994) and ServerStat (1995) for Web servers also began to appear, allowing us to analyze server logs to see who was accessing the library's Web server, what HTML pages were being accessed most often, what days and times of week and month were busiest for the server, etc. At first most of the hits on our server came from educational and government institutions with a ratio of three to one when compared to commercial sites, but as time went on, this ratio reversed itself as more commercial sites started to appear and access our Web server. A whole new dimension of commerce began to develop across the Internet. Internet marketing and market analysis began to open up within just a year or two after Mosaic was released. Other Web browsers appeared briefly and died. Marc Andreessen, who had headed the creative team responsible for Mosaic, formed his own commercial firm, Netscape. With another team of young, bright programmers, he created the most popular Web browser on the Net today.

STAFF TRAINING BECOMES A PRIORITY

By August 1994, one year after installing our first 56k line to the Internet for reference staff use, our library staff began to provide Internet Access for public use on an experimental basis. We used one of the Macintosh computers at the main library that we had originally purchased for public access to our Community Connection database. We did this without any fanfare and gave no public service announcement about it, but with this workstation SJCPL became the first public library in Indiana to provide such direct public access.

The idea all along was to offer Internet access to the public, but before we could do that at any more of our public workstations, we needed to see how the public might react. And more importantly, we had to train our staff. In that same month, we hired an Internet training specialist, Faith Fleming, a professional librarian who taught Internet use at Cornell University. Ms. Fleming's job description and first assignment was to train our professional and paraprofessional staff in the reference uses of the Internet, working with Joyce Hug. Faith and Joyce worked hard selling the Internet as a reference tool to our librarians. They also lobbied the administration for a place for the staff to practice their skills. Soon we created a staff training room with five workstations in a nonpublic area. All professional and paraprofessional staff were encouraged to take time each week to spend an hour or two in the training room. In addition, Ms. Fleming and Ms. Hug presented Internet-related lessons at staff meetings. It took the improvements in Web browsers and the response time of the new T-1 line to sell the staff on using the Internet for reference questions. Another very big plus for the reference staff was getting access to the Internet from every terminal at the reference desk.

Once most of the reference staff was somewhat comfortable, we prepared to offer what we had to the public. We had started in August 1994 with the one Internet Macintosh at the back of our bank of CD-ROM workstations. This was in use constantly, and we found that we had to install security software. Next we set up a cluster of three Macintosh computer workstations across from our main library Information and Reference desk, which we named "The Internet Connection" (borrowed from Quarterman and Carl-Mitchell, 1994). Along with these stations came Internet workstations in our Children's Room and our Magazine Department. At the Internet Connection we offered telnet, Gopher, Archie, ftp, and Mosaic.

THE INTEGRATING FORCE OF THE INTERNET

In the fall of 1995, while working again at the main library Reference & Information desk, I tried to answer reference questions by jumping back and forth among three different networked terminals or computer workstations. Access to our online catalog was provided for the most part through dumb terminals connected to our mainframe with dedicated lines; our Internet workstations also provided access through Web browsers with a telnet link from our home page. Access to our CD-ROM tower and its CD-ROM databases was provided through several IBM-compatible computer workstations connected by a local area network (LAN). Because of software limitations, we could not give the branch libraries access to this CD-ROM network. Access to the Internet was through our Macintosh computer workstations linked through an Ethernet/router system to our T-1 line.

Running from platform to platform and network to network to answer reference questions seemed ridiculous. After four hours of doing this, I resolved to plan with my staff another migration to one fully integrated network of

Internet protocols on one common platform, and to make this available first at every reference desk and next at every public workstation. At the time we had about 150 terminals or workstations on these three different networks. Based on our budget, we developed a plan to replace one third of them (fifty) per year with intelligent workstations over a three-year period, and to upgrade our online catalog software. With the upgrade to a T-1 line to the Internet and 64k lines to the branches late in 1995, we were able to add many more workstations, which we dubbed "infostations." Most of these were within sight of our reference desk. Like the CD-ROM workstations that they replaced, the infostations were placed in clusters of four machines, two facing each other. Initially, each pair shared a printer.

The introduction of WebPac by Innovative Interfaces and the burgeoning of Internet access to magazine indices and full-text articles with products like Infotrac permitted some common interfaces. The availability on the Web of leased information products which were formerly only available in CD-ROM formats suggested further items to be interfaced. We completed this integration by the summer of 1998 to the point where we now have nearly all of our electronic databases integrated into one Web browser interface at intelligent workstations for both staff and public. We have also exchanged our ink jet printers, which were a constant source of maintenance problems, for faster, more reliable, and better quality laser printers that are networked to one location in our main library and in our branches. This gives us better control of hard-copy production.

Only a few of the leased CD-ROM databases now remain on our CD-ROM tower. We now have Web-based access to General Business File and *Encyclopedia Britannica*, in addition to EbscoHost and UMI's full-text Newspaper Database, which includes the *South Bend Tribune* and other major Indiana papers along with the *Chicago Tribune*, *The New York Times*, *USA Today*, and *The Wall Street Journal*, which was added recently. We also have college catalogs in a Web-based product and Electric Library which has full-text articles from various sources and is excellent for homework assignments.

FURTHER TRAINING AND STAFF DEVELOPMENT

In May of 1996, on a long-range planning retreat of our administrative and system coordinators, we determined that our increasingly rapid change was creating understandable stress for our staff. Much more emphasis needed to be placed on training and development. We needed to improve and build up their self-confidence. They needed better planning and management tools with which to work. We wanted to improve interpersonal relationships and develop team spirit and camaraderie in and between departments. Assistant Director Debra Futa, who led the staff team that developed our primary role as an "information hub of the community," advocated this approach. She provided strong leadership to move us in this direction. As a result of that first planning session and later discussions with our department heads and their staffs, we created a staff-training plan. We were guided by a planning consultant, Sharon Wiseman, from Prospect Heights, Illinois. The plan included the training of our administrative and top management staff in Dr. Stephen R. Covey's *Seven Habits of Highly Effective People* (1989). All of the administrators and coordinators first went through the three-and-one-half-day Covey course and followed that with the four-day course to become licensed facilitators of the Seven Habits program. The first step, in other words, was to "train the trainers," and then have the administrators and coordinators (including the director) train the rest of the staff.

By fall 1998 we had trained 180 staff members in the Seven Habits. To improve and deepen our understanding of the Seven Habits, we have also asked our staff to go through the Myers Briggs Type Indicator (MBTI) testing and analysis program. Working with our consultant, each branch and department discussed the results of their tests in order to learn to understand and appreciate each other's differences (a Covey principle) with the aim of developing stronger, nurturing teams and generating staff creativity to meet the challenges of a rapidly changing work environment. We anticipate the development of a set of core values peculiar to our profession and public service commitment. We expect a new vision statement to emerge. Customer service and satisfaction will be our top priorities as we design the next phase of staff training.

NETWORK RESOURCES
DEVELOPMENT TRAINING TEAM (NRDS)

In 1997 we consolidated our staff training efforts by creating a new service department, Networked Resources Development Training Team, with Michael Stephens as our training specialist and Joyce Hug as our Web specialist.

NRDT (or Nerdts, as it is affectionately called) now specializes in continuous training of our professional and paraprofessional staff in the use of our networked electronic resources, including the Internet. Staff members who attend "Train the Trainers" sessions in turn offer training programs for the public. We learned from Covey that the best way to learn is to teach it to others, and to do so on a regular basis.

The next step is to integrate our computer workstations with our telephone services through unified voice messaging. This will help integrate our communications devices, information resources, and protocols. The reference librarian will be able to find the answer to any question, in any source, in any format, from anywhere in the world. She can also transmit that information through any means of communication to the user, by voice, visual, e-mail, fax, ftp, telnet, or Web telephony.

Before we can begin to do this, however, the staff must first learn and become comfortable with this new multifaceted approach to providing customer service. Like that first Macintosh SLIP connection, we will start by experimenting with the possibilities in a back room or in the NRDT Department. We will demonstrate, discuss, and share experiences with our professional staff, and then develop a training program before placing such services at our reference desks. Administrators also need to become familiar with this new way of transacting business through one interface in order to find ways of extending their own management, communicating, training, and coaching skills with their staffs.

TRAINING THE PUBLIC

Within less than a year after providing that first Macintosh computer with public access to the Internet, Faith Fleming, Joyce Hug, and reference librarian Michael Stephens were teaching not only the staff but also the public about the uses of the Internet as an information resource through "The Internet Connection," a program developed by Ms. Fleming.

Beginning March 1995, our classes and demonstrations covered Internet basics and were designed for people with some computer experience. Both beginner and advanced courses were offered three times per month at the main library and once monthly at one of our largest branches. At the branch library the first basic class took place during a blizzard, yet still managed to draw fifty attendees. Extending the series in 1996, we attracted about two hundred people to the main library over a three-night period. Following the success of this series, we went on to schedule Internet instructional programs once every month, refining the offerings to include "special topics" which focused on subject-specific classes dealing with business on the Internet, mailing lists, and job searching resources on the Web. Other subjects such as Basic HTML, Using Search Engines, and such topics as Gardening Sites, Travel Resources, College and Career Resources, and Business and Finance were presented. These remain very popular and are well attended.

With the addition of ten new workstations in a public area near the main library reference desk (spring 1998), we now also offer regular, continuing hands-on Internet sessions for the public. The classes are an hour and a half long and are for people with little or no computer skills. We have sessions every other Saturday morning and every other Wednesday afternoon. We cover basic Netscape navigation and search engines, and run through our Internet resources from our Hotlist. A rotating pool of our reference librarians teaches the classes. This sharpens their skills, and establishes our librarians as the Internet experts in our community. We have offered these sessions to many area clubs, business organizations, and social agencies. Again, we are seen as the "Information Hub" for our community, the primary role of our current Mission Statement. Among those who have asked for special sessions were a group of reporters from our local newspaper, the *South Bend Tribune*, the Investment Association, Rotary, Kiwanis, and homeschoolers.

Joyce Hug created our first Hotlist, which now serves as our default page in Netscape for all public computers at our main library and branches. On March 14, 1998, the fourth anniversary of our original Web page on the Internet, Joyce introduced us to a completely revamped home page with the use of Java scripts, a new Intranet for staff communications, and several new interactive forums. Most recently, the Adult Reference & Information staff also introduced our new interactive online Electronic Reference service to the public.

We now have a committee of reference librarians to recommend sites and organize our Hotlist. They have a selection role similar to the one they have enjoyed with books. This is a wonderful way of organizing the Internet for reference use and of getting the staff involved in the Internet. Our Hotlist is a helpful way to guide patrons to the useful sites on the Web, and it is the first thing our public sees when they open up Netscape on our infostations.

Our staff currently provides basic start-up assistance, troubleshooting, and limited help with search strategies at our public desks. We limit our staff to about twenty minutes with each patron, less if there are other patrons waiting. Patrons have a two-hour per day limit on the infostations. There is a one-hour limit on the computers when others are waiting, and on Sundays the limits are cut in half. We make no distinction between adult and juvenile users, except that our children's room is limited to children only.

SJCPL began providing Internet access as an information tool for its reference librarians as early as September 1992. Today we offer Internet access to the general public on over fifty infostations at the main library and seven branches. Our main library alone has over thirty infostations, and we are adding new stations each year in a three-year planning cycle to replace one-third of our computer workstations as the technology changes. Currently most of our infostations are Apple Power Mac 7200 and G3 platforms. Internet access to the main library is provided by a T-1 line, with 64k dedicated digital lines going out to the seven branches from the main library. These lines not only provide Internet access but also data transmission for our Innovative Interfaces automated system. We have plans to add a second T-1 line from the main library to the Internet that will work in tandem with our current T-1 line. In addition to the current 64K lines from the main library to our larger branches, we will be adding five T-1 lines, one for each of these busier branches.

SHARING WITH THE COMMUNITY

Just as our county library system was about to have installed its first 56K in the fall of 1993, a small group of local businessmen who wanted to start a community-based computer network approached us. Don McLaughlin, the leader of the group, called it "our community's access ramp to the information superhighway." Don, a local stockbroker working for A. G. Edwards, Inc. had become an Internet user himself through a home computer and his own connections at the University of Notre Dame. He had an avid interest in electronic music and found he could acquire some great digital sound files by ftp over the Internet.

Don McLaughlin became the founding father of what was to become known as Michiana Free-Net (http://michiana.org/). With SJCPL's assistance, Michiana Free-Net (MFN) put up its first Web page on the SJCPL Web server on August 26, 1994. With seed money from MCI ($53,000) and a grant

($32,000) from Access Indiana Information Network (http://www. state.in.us/), Michiana Free-Net was able to purchase its own Web server early in 1996. By May of that year, MFN began taking subscribers as Indiana's first Free-Net, providing services to over 500 residents. Since then MFN has become an important resource to the Michiana community, serving St. Joseph and Elkhart Counties of northern Indiana and parts of lower Michigan, benefiting its users with links as broad as national and international information services and as narrow as their local friends and neighbors. Michiana Free-Net still has its Web server housed in SJCPL's main library computer room and contracts with SJCPL as its Internet Service Provider. With the technical expertise of Joyce Hug as its Web site specialist and the business management skills of Steve Ross, its CEO, Michiana Free-Net has become one of the most successful not-for-profit community nets in the United States, with nearly 1,800 subscribers and about 96 phone lines.

SJCPL BECOMES AN INTERNET SERVICE PROVIDER

In September 1995, just before migrating from our GEAC system to a new Innovative Interfaces automated system, SJCPL upgraded its 56K line to a T-1 and installed seven 64k lines from its main library to all its branch libraries. Later that year three other Indiana public libraries (Mishawaka-Penn Public Library, Plymouth Public Library, and the Bremen Public Library) that contract with SJCPL for their automated services also joined our Internet cluster with four more 64K lines to our main library. Finally, Michiana Free-Net contracted with SJCPL, locating their new Internet server at our main library and connecting directly into our new T-1 line. SJCPL negotiated a new contract with CICNet, Inc. which enabled SJCPL to become a reseller of Internet access to these and similar nonprofit entities. This made SJCPL one of the first public libraries in the United States to become an Internet Service Provider as well as a user.

SJCPL CREATES THE PLA'S
FIRST NATIONAL CONFERENCE WEB SITE

At the 1995 ALA Annual Conference in June, as a member of the Public Library Associations Board of Directors and a member of the PLA National

Conference Program Planning Committee, I volunteered to have SJCPL create and host on one of our Web servers the PLA Web site for its 1996 National Conference in Portland, Oregon, March 26–30, 1996. The PLA Board and Planning Committee accepted my offer and the very first PLA national conference Web pages appeared on the Net in the fall of 1995, providing service to the profession from our Web server in South Bend, Indiana. CICNet provided SJCPL with an additional proxy name, "pla.org," for its server address in South Bend. All of the important lessons and skills we learned in maintaining our own Web pages were brought to bear on this new, important responsibility for PLA, including the use of tables, clickable maps, animated GIFs, interactive forums, predetermined page, column, and font sizes for conference registration forms, etc. The ability to locate a Web server anywhere in the world to serve another organization in another part of the world and make it appear that it was coming from that organization was another important lesson for us. We even found it possible to create Web pages with images that came from another Web server, such as those among PLA's conference tour companies. The use of the Internet as a tool for collaboration between organizations and sites throughout the world opened up new vistas for us.

SJCPL BECOMES KNOWN WORLDWIDE

During this entire period of time SJCPL also enjoyed the publicity that being a leader on the Web brought. Several of our staff members contributed articles to professional journals (Blacharski, 1998; Hug & Fleming, 1995). SJCPL was recognized nationally for its Web home page (Streitfeld, 1995; Raeder, 1995). Thanks to the efforts of staff members like Linda Broyles, Joyce Hug, Nancy Korpal, Dave Haslett, and Faith Fleming, SJCPL was recognized as a national "success story" by the United States Advisory Council on the National Information Infrastructure (NIIAC). In the NIIAC final report to President Clinton and Vice-President Gore, titled "KickStart Initiative: Connecting America's Communities to the Information Superhighway," SJCPL was also recognized by the American Library Association's Office for Research and Statistics report, "Profiles of Public Library Internet Projects," for its innovative work and "no grants, just guts" attitude in being the first in the U.S. to provide Web access to the public.

Finally, in addition to all that we have said about the people on our staff who made this all possible, special mention needs to be given to staff members such as Dave Haslett, head of Computer Services; Nancy Korpal, former head of Technical Services and now head of Main Library Adult Services; and Linda Broyles, "the Mother" of nearly all of our local databases, for the outstanding work they and their technical staff have done in keeping up with constant upgrades in equipment and software throughout this seven-year period. Without the positive "Let's get it done!" attitude, we could never have come as far as we have.

SJCPL Now and Tomorrow

Where are we now, after being active on the Web for seven years? The following list of changes at SJCPL are either recently accomplished or about to be accomplished:

- Five T-1 lines are to be added to the five busiest branch libraries (these five branches will retain their present 64k lines which will continue to handle only Innovative Interfaces data transmissions; all other Internet traffic will go over the new T-1 lines on new separate routers).
- A T-1 linked the main library to the University of Notre Dame with a second T-1 planned.
- Over 50 Infostations systemwide provide Internet access to the public.
- Over 160 staff computers had access to the Internet.
- Two free public Internet classes are offered per month: The second Monday is "Introduction to the Internet" and the fourth Monday is "Special Topics."
- Four free hands-on training sessions are taught for the public per month.
- Our own mail server has over 100 e-mail accounts.
- Internet access was extended to three cluster libraries with over 100 public and staff Internet computers.
- Two Web servers had over 12,000 hits per day.
- One staff Intranet is accessible to all branches and departments that contains important internal information in electronic form.
- One ftp server exists.
- Seven leased databases are accessed over the Web.

- A Web version of our online catalog is offered.
- An electronic reference service lets people ask questions over the Internet.
- Housing and support for Michiana Free-Net are given with 1,800 users and 96 phone lines.
- Five in-house databases are accessible from the Internet.
- An extensive staff training program with eight Internet classes is offered each month. In addition, special departmental and branch sessions are offered to handle specific Internet/electronic questions.
- An entirely new department called Networked Resources/ Development Training, with one full-time trainer and one full-time Web specialist is being created.

Lessons Learned

In retrospect, would we have done anything differently? We probably should have gone to a 56k line connection immediately, making the Internet available to more of our professional librarians sooner so that they were all better prepared. Although we quietly installed that first public access computer to the Internet, we should have begun staff training at least six months prior. We also should have planned on the full integration of access to all of all our databases before purchasing more terminals and before upgrading our CD-ROM tower. We did not know, however, how the technology would develop. We did our best, taking advantage of what was available and where the technology seemed to be moving at the time. This is really all one can expect from anyone in this fast-changing environment. Overall, there is not much that we would or could have changed. We are very thankful to the University of Notre Dame for their support, to CICNet, to Michiana Free-Net, to our Automated Cluster members, and to the many, many individuals and staff members who worked hard and long to get us where we are.

Where is SJCPL going and do public libraries have a future? No one is certain where the Internet will take us. Some of the best thinkers in the world, I am told, cannot predict where this new world of instant multimedia communication will lead. Certainly national boundaries will diminish, and distance will have no meaning with respect to education, commerce, and access to information. Public libraries, we think, will continue to be the public's broker for access to information in all its formats as long as we make it very user-friendly, client-centered, and economical. These are very exciting times. What does the future hold when the most creative minds in the world can talk to each other, instantly and constantly, at any time and can share their thoughts with the rest of the world? No one can tell. Everything will certainly move even faster as this creativity feeds on itself.

If SJCPL's staff and Library Board can continue to respond to rapid changes as well as they have over the past seven years, then I have no fear about the future for public libraries. So long as we continue to focus on service and the needs of others, and we engender in our plans and efforts the values of our mission statement to "solve problems, spark curiosity, and inspire dreams," public support will be there, and SJCPL will continue to create its own future as a key participant and leader in meeting the information needs of its community.

Acknowledgments

The writing of this chapter was a team project. I am indebted to my co-authors including Joyce Hug (Networked Resources/Web Site Specialist), Joe Sipocz (head of Adult Reference & Information Services, main library), and Michael Stephens (Networked Resources/Staff Trainer). The following staff also made contributions: Debra Futa (Assistant Director), Linda Broyles (Networking Systems Coordinator), and David Haslett (head of Automated Services).

References

Blacharski, D. (1998, April/May). Library users gain instant access to databases via the Web. *FileMaker Pro Advisor*, 20-24.

Covey, S. R. (1989). *The seven habits of highly effective people: Restoring the character ethic*. New York: Simon & Schuster.

Hug, J. & Fleming, F. (1995, Winter). Internet basics for reference. *Indiana Libraries*, 51-63.

Nelson, T. H. (1981). *Literary machines*. Swarthmore, PA: Ted Nelson.

Quarterman, J. S. & Carl-Mitchell, S. (1994). *The Internet connection: System connectivity and configuration*. Reading, MA: Addison-Wesley.

Raeder, A. (1995, April). The Internet express: Visiting libraries via the Internet. *Searcher: The Magazine for Database Professionals, 3* (4), 8-140.

Streitfeld, D. (1995, August 28). Cash-strapped libraries discover life on-line. *The Washington Post*, A01, A09.

School Libraries Meet the Tornadoes:
The Transformational Impact of School Reform and the Web

Joyce Kasman Valenza
Librarian
Springfield Township High School
Erdenheim, Pennsylvania

"Toto, I have a feeling we're not in Kansas anymore!"
—Dorothy, picking herself up

THE FORECAST

A series of powerful twisters are blowing through our school libraries. The two strongest of the winds—school reform and technology—have just about blown the roofs off. And like Dorothy, we must get up, dust off our skirts (and slacks!) and realize that these winds transport us to places both challenging and delightful. Such places offer us new opportunities to use the skills and perspective we've spent years developing. Like Dorothy, we may be compelled to leave comfortable, possibly complacent roles to reaffirm or assume new roles as leaders and learners and guides. Like Dorothy, we are discovering that we have landed in confusing new surroundings, and we must now set direction for ourselves and others. We are discovering a new potential to create yellow brick roads—roads that will lead students and teachers to the destinations they most need to visit, will encourage thought, and will prove that the journey is every bit as important as the destination.

What would we see if we could peer over the rainbow? My vision of the future is a merging of the best of the Emerald City and the best of the traditions of back home. It involves productive and creative use of the transformational information and communication technology around us—the Web specifically—with a couple of very old "killer apps"—a devotion to literacy and a commitment to learning. It is a clear vision of school librarians as leaders. As the storms settle, we need to evaluate the changing turf, set a course, link arms with our friends, and forge ahead. Do we drift around in a balloon or control the action knowledgeably using our ruby slippers? I say we "choose the shoes." Our challenge is to prepare students for productive use of the vast information arena before them.

Who Are Our Students?

Today's students were born into a post-PC, fast-food world. It is likely they do not remember a time when ATMs did not conveniently deliver cash and their own computers did not deliver information. The technology tornado has had a broad reach, affecting the way we all work. The privileged among our students, and their parents, are used to information delivery via the Web and their CD-ROMs at home, or anywhere, 7 x 24 hours. Will this liberate them from the need to use a library altogether? If we define libraries narrowly as information providers, perhaps. If we define libraries by the physical space they occupy, perhaps. But access does not equal understanding. And access to information is a long way from effective communication of ideas. Students, even those well used to self-service information, require and deserve guidance. We now have the tools to expand that guidance well beyond our walls and traditional hours.

Will School Libraries Survive the Twisters?

School libraries can define libraries for our future citizens. If students understand the impact a library can have in improving information access and the impact librarians have in providing guidance, libraries should thrive. If school libraries become true learning environments, providing human advice, intervention between technologies and people, both online and off, students will continue to use libraries as adults. But students must see that information dissemination and retrieval is but the beginning of a larger process, and that technology cannot be separated from process. In the shadow of the Web, in the quest for speedy service, the quiet, thoughtful work of research cannot be overlooked. So if we are to examine the way in which the

Internet has affected the school library landscape, we must also examine the way in which it must be used. Learning environments are changing in a fundamental way. Enter Tornado One.

Tornado One: Educational Reform

The wizards of the educational community have long been suggesting that there are better ways to ensure that all of our students learn. Contemporary learning theorists have led us to question traditional pedagogy and to rethink our methods of measuring success. A new understanding of learning, based on brain research, urges teachers to appreciate individual learning styles and recognize multiple intelligences. Our schools are moving from an instructionist to a constructivist approach.

This approach is perfect for a technology-rich school environment in which the librarian is a major player. Constructivist learners solve authentic, or real-life problems. They make predictions, or hypotheses, to be tested or proven through research. The approach focuses on inquiry. Students are encouraged to develop their own driving, or essential questions and investigate solutions using raw data, primary sources, and physical, interactive materials. The learner is at the center of a dynamic process, not simply absorbing but also constructing knowledge while collaborating with peers. Projects often cross disciplines. Student inquiry leaps naturally from science to social studies to math. Students and teachers engage in active discussion as they build on each other's ideas and create and present their solutions. Teachers provide access to resources, and guide as students set their own learning goals.

Implications for the School Library

Theorists in the information field contend that the information search process mirrors this description of the learning process: students actively seek to construct meaning from the sources they encounter and to create products that shape and communicate that meaning effectively. Core elements in both learning and information theory thus converge to suggest that developing expertise in accessing, evaluating, and using information is in fact the authentic learning that modern education seeks to promote (see *Information Literacy Standards for Student Learning*, 1998).

This resource-based approach encourages students to move well beyond their textbooks to examine authentic literature: journal articles, videos, books, interviews, Web sites, and documents. Students are challenged to reach beyond factual response—to analyze, compare, defend, and create. And learning is viewed as nonlinear, recursive, a progression of skills to be revisited and enhanced. The learning community is no longer limited by age or place or occupation or content area. Learners are linked by common interests. These strategies are all about what good research and library work always were. They present the perfect climate for students to practice information skills. Searching is all about problem solving.

These trends in addressing the needs of learners require a logistical shift. The authentic investigations of students, their Web searching and multimedia production for instance, cannot be comfortably squeezed into forty-five-minute chunks of time. Efforts in reform are being logistically translated into block schedules in many of our secondary schools, creating focused longer periods of time for students to spend in each of their classes. Block scheduling creates the perfect opportunity for collaborating across disciplines and carves out the real time needed for students to conduct effective research and create better products. In our elementary schools the demands of an inquiry and resource-based curriculum cannot be met if the school library schedule remains fixed and the school library information specialist remains a convenient "prep time" drop off for teachers. Separated from the real work of the classroom, old-fashioned "library time" becomes irrelevant.

All of these current pedagogical trends point directly to strong libraries. But they point to an evolved vision of the school library. The center of curriculum, the over-the-rainbow library, is the model of the restructured classroom—a laboratory where communities of learners meet; where teachers come to plan collaboratively; where everyone is a welcome learner; where learners pursue their own questions; where multiple learning styles are addressed; where diversity is both recognized and celebrated. The new school library offers adequate, flexible space; an open schedule and guidance for multidisciplinary and multi-age activities and for truly meaningful research. The over-the-rainbow library is well funded and well staffed. In the over-the-rainbow library the librarian is also a scout, learning about emerging technologies, mastering strategies for managing information resources while modeling activities that inspire greater learning.

This new climate demands strong teacher/librarian partnerships. To further the learning process, librarians must work with teachers as partners to create new types of assignments for students. If students are to be problem solvers, they need real problems. The old questions no longer work. Online access to basic information has made answering the easy questions easier. It is no longer valuable (it may never have been!) to ask a child to do a report on a president. If you asked me to write one, I might respond that the *World Book* editors have already done a far better job than I ever could. Why replicate their excellent work? But ask me to decide and defend my findings on which twentieth century president did the most to promote civil rights. Ahhh! There's a project that would force me to not only locate information, but to analyze it, evaluate it, communicate it—indeed, understand it! Student work should now forge well beyond information location and the fill-in-the-blank work sheet. In our heavily Web-based, knowledge society, citizens need to solve real information problems. Our new questions should challenge students to locate the best information from the enormous pool of data and to actually use that to build new understanding. School assignments are, or should be, shifting from worksheets and fact-finding reports to problem solving.

There has been an enormous shift in the way we approach learning, and all of it points directly to the student-centered school library. The shift points to the school librarian as teacher, instructional partner, information specialist, and program administrator. But the shift is only the beginning of the story. Look out for Tornado Two.

Tornado Two: Explosion of Information Technology

The Web has changed everything. Used well, it can be a catalyst to transform education. The Web can provide an information-rich environment of ambiguity and complexity to challenge our students. The Web can engage communities of learners in problem-based, authentic research, but this won't happen if we happen fail to recognize the connection between Tornado One and Tornado Two. There are those who say that classroom Internet availability will eliminate the need for a school library. My crystal ball forecasts dire consequences if the personal link between technology and the student is removed. Indeed, virtual libraries are needed because they expand our guidance and provide greater access. But our physical presence is critical; at no time before have school librarians been more needed.

A Remarkable Tornado!

For the first time our students are faced with global, unfiltered perspectives. The Internet offers first-hand information from thousands of people with thousands of different backgrounds—political, racial, ethnic, economic. If there are two sides to an issue, both will be represented. If there are 300 sides to an issue, they'll all be represented. Basically every interest imaginable is represented, creating a chaotic, yet democratic, open forum. Publishing was once limited to a few authors and journalists; now everyone's ideas can be read, viewed, heard or ignored.

The Internet provides access to breaking news. Online news services like CNN, with its up-to-the-minute reports, have dramatically raised our expectations for current information. Newspapers, magazines, even television and radio cannot put the news up as quickly. Access to information is now available twenty-four-hour-a-day/seven-days-a-week. It is there at your convenience, from wherever you log on, on demand and in a variety of media formats —real video, real audio, graphics, live images, transcripts.

One of the true bonuses of Web use in the schools is the availability of primary sources. Primary sources allow students to use their analytical skills in historic inquiry. Through such collections as those of the National Digital Library, the Smithsonian, and the National Archives and Records Administration, students and teachers have easy access to documents: legislations, photographs, oral histories, and letters. Through the digitized collections of our fine museums, students and teachers can create their own exhibits, placing pieces of art they could never physically visit side by side for comparison.

The Internet provides access to people, with opportunities for interaction that traditional texts could never offer; in fact, the Internet encourages this interaction and communication. Students can easily e-mail the Webmaster of any page they find valuable to get further information. "E-mail is underrated," says Peter Milbury, librarian at Chico High School in California. "It is information in its most powerful and dense form. It is very personal, almost the opposite of the Web, but equally powerful for students to use as an information source."

Taming the Winds

To ensure that our students and our faculty are effective users of information in this rich information environment is truly an energizing challenge. School librarians are trying to rise to the occasion, organizing the information for students and faculty and offering guidance in searching, analyzing, evaluating, using, and communicating information. We now have the opportunity to teach truly useful, immediately applicable searching skills. We have never been in a better position to help our users.

Imagine receiving a gift of ruby slippers. You might enjoy showing them off. You'd want to slip them on right away. Though shiny and attractive, they'd be of little use without knowledge and experience. Dorothy's ruby slippers did her little good until she discovered how to use them and understood where she wanted them to take her. Like ruby slippers, Internet in our classrooms has proven not to be "plug and play." True integration and effective use takes understanding and careful planning.

In technology-rich schools, school librarians play a pivotal role. We have always taught information skills, but the need for those skills has never been as urgent because information has never been more available or more difficult to manage. Surfing and searching are two entirely different paths. Technology has improved access to information and our ability to communicate, but mastery of information skills goes far beyond access and effective communication goes far beyond connection.

Ten years ago I was eager to share my knowledge of searching with students. With those small CD-ROM databases, students generally got where they wanted to be through a simple title search or by selecting a couple of obvious keywords. Though I tried to interest students in the power of searching the DIALOG databases, few ever got past the unattractive text interface.

The vast and uneven Web has made the need for skills far more apparent to teachers and more critical to students. Suddenly, others have a new appreciation of what we offer. Even those who say they are confident using the Internet really still have a lot to learn. As the information technology specialist in the school, librarians provide training to both staff and students in emerging information technologies. Our users need the order we can create through our pathfinders and bookmarks and Web pages. They need our guidance in preparing a search offline; selecting the best search tools; learning the difference between search engines and subject directories; the importance of phrase searching and exactly how to use Boolean operators. Among the many available choices, they need to learn how to find the best resources to help them solve a particular problem. Often our guidance must lead students to look beyond the single interface of the Web to pay services. Our guidance must also lead them back to subject-specific CD-ROMs, journals and books. Yes, books! And well beyond location, we must offer guided practice in evaluating, analyzing, and communicating information effectively in a technology-rich environment.

Evaluation Is Critical

Not all the good stuff is packaged as obviously as the lovely good witch, Glinda. Perhaps the biggest of our challenges in working with students on the Web is training them to carefully evaluate their sources. For some students, access to information technology has created a false impression that all they will ever need will be contained in a quick printout. Our collections will present an increasing number of choices—so many places to start. Choosing among the Web, several online pay services, CD-ROM, journals, and books is an overwhelming task. Without both group and individual guidance, students are very likely to overlook the best sources.

Packaging is important to our mediacentric kids. The beautifully Java-interactive, one-page Web site may be far more appealing than the lengthy biography which took a noted author three years of careful research and analysis to complete. Our shelves of copyrighted nonfiction may never make it to the Web. Will they be completely overlooked? Our work with teachers must include developing an understanding of balance in research. What is quality content? What is merely fluff and sound bytes? What is of no value at all? Without heavy book-talking and encouragement, valuable traditional resources will be increasingly overlooked.

I believe that this evaluation skill is so critical that I approach it as the very first activity in orientation. I seek out the most unreliable Web page I can find, display it, and ask for student opinion. Students are generally easily impressed by a page that has a few graphics and appears to have sufficient content to help them with a report. I ask them to "interview" the page and develop criteria for assessing it. Building on their own participation, they establish a need to examine: authorship, date, accuracy, source of information, relevance. I often stop a class for a "five-minute huddle" to examine some of their Web discoveries.

Our colleagues, Kathy Schrock (http://www.capecod.net/schrockguide/) and Linda Joseph (*Net Curriculum: An Educator's Guide to Using the Internet*), offer some excellent tools for students to use in their evaluation of Web resources (see Figure 7.1).

CRITICAL EVALUATION OF A WEB SITE : ELEMENTARY SCHOOL LEVEL

c1996 Kathleen Schrock (kschrock@capecod.net)
Kathy Schrock's Guide for Educators -- http://www.capecod.net/schrockguide/

1. How are you hooked to the Internet? ___ Computer and modem ___ Direct connection at school

2. If you are using a modem, what is the speed? 2400 -- 9600 -- 14.4 -- 28.8 -- 33.6 -- 56k

3. What Web browser are you using? _____

4. What is the URL of the Web page you are looking at?

http:// _____

5. What is the name of the site? _____

How Does It Look?

Does the page take a long time to load?   YES / NO

Are there big pictures on the page?   YES / NO

Is the spelling correct on the page?   YES / NO

Is the author's name and e-mail address on the page?   YES / NO

Is there a picture on the page that you can use
to choose links? (Image map)   YES / NO

Is there information in columns on the page? (Table)   YES / NO

If you go to another page, is there a way to get back to the first page?   YES / NO

Is there a date that tells you when the page was made?   YES / NO

Do the photographs look real?   YES / NO / NO PHOTOGRAPHS

Do the sounds sound real?   YES / NO / NO SOUNDS

What Did You Learn?

Does the title of the page tell you what it is about?   YES / NO

Is there an introduction on the page that tells you what is included?   YES / NO

Are the facts on the page what you were looking for?   YES / NO

Would you have gotten more information from the encyclopedia? YES / NO

Would the information have been better in the encyclopedia?   YES / NO

Does the author of the page say some things you disagree with?   YES / NO

Does the author of the page include information that you know is wrong?   YES / NO

Do the pictures and photographs on the page help you learn?   YES / NO / NO PICTURES

Summary

Looking at all of the questions and answers above, write a sentence telling why this Web site is helpful (or not helpful) for your project.

_____

_____

_____

Figure 7.1

CREATING GOOD CITIZENS OF OZ

Often as a lone voice, school librarians recognize and respond to the social issues of Web use in their libraries. Students need to learn their own responsibility as citizens in a digital world—what it means to respect intellectual property and copyright, why equity of access is important, and what it means to use technology responsibly. School librarians are quickly becoming consultants on how to battle plagiarism, maintain the integrity of student work, handle citations in ever-emerging formats, and manage permissions for use of outside materials in student multimedia projects and Web pages.

The introduction of electronic reference has generated a growing concern about plagiarism in our schools. Most children cannot envision the dark ages—the world of the yellow pad, index card, and erasable typing paper. Composing and editing text has come a long way since our own college days. There is danger and temptation out there. And many students are taking too much advantage of the flexible nature of digital text. Students are not just editing their own text. They are editing the text of others, calling it their own, and calling it research. Voilà! It is now very easy to piece together a term paper from materials culled from a few Web sites or CD-ROM sources. Teachers once adept at identifying sources from the limited print materials available are confounded by the sheer number of possible sources from which their students may have borrowed, unless they innocently point to them in their bibliographies. Few students choose to provide those leads. One ninth grader told me, "There are so many sources out there, that it's impossible for a teacher to tell if a student plagiarized. The Internet has made it easy."

Students need to know and we need to consistently teach: Anytime you take the words, ideas or creative work of another and claim them as your own, you are plagiarizing. This means text and images and sounds and video. Of course, they may use the works of others as long as they credit the source. But any direct quote, image, sound, and video that is copied must be cited. Issues of intellectual property are complicated. There are areas of gray, and students and teachers are confused. Instruction in information ethics should begin as early as students begin to write.

Children should understand that intellectual property is still property. Though the threat of consequences may be a powerful deterrent, the real deterrent should be ethical. Copying the work of others is wrong. As easy and as tempting as it may be in an electronic information environment, plagiarizing is cheating.

School librarians must take a leadership position in this instruction as well as a position in developing the policies for use of information technology in their districts. No other staff member is as qualified to develop a policy for responsible use of information or to discuss and defend issues relating to intellectual freedom in the electronic environment. No other staff member is as qualified to help students understand the increasingly complicated issues of intellectual property and plagiarism as students produce multimedia or design Web pages. No other staff member is as uniquely qualified to see the whole spectrum of sources and guide students to best choices. No other facility will ensure the kind of technology equity a library can. Drop-in access before or after school, when labs are booked by classes, ensures that those who do not have access at home have convenient access at school.

But What of Product?

Technology will have continual impact on the way students communicate the results of their research. Business people are not passing term papers around board rooms. They make presentations using state-of-the-art multimedia tools, and they post their sales pitches on their Web pages. Multimedia production, increasingly Web-published, is the communication of research. As the culmination of the research process, it must be a part of the library's program. It makes perfect sense—students cannot produce quality products without content. I have seen projects produced by students working exclusively in multimedia labs. Of course, these labs offer the hardware and the software and some networked reference materials to allow students to put together a glitzy presentation, but students need a fusion of resources—journals, recordings, reference books, the Internet, CD-ROMs—all of which are conveniently accessible in only one place. Students need advice on how to structure their projects, how to develop a thesis, how to treat various types of information in citation. Students need time to drop in to work on these projects before and after school. And faculty involved in multimedia projects need partners to complement their skills and to offer students both subject specialist and process advice. A librarian with updated skills is uniquely qualified to pull all of this together and relate these information literacy skills to content area learning, thereby making an essential contribution to the learning process. So the over-the-rainbow library must have areas for production with the appropriate equipment and peripherals—scanners, digital cameras—and flexible space.

COLLECTION BUILDING AND ACCESS TO INFORMATION

We are faced with continually evolving choices in selecting resources. Newer software developments will continue to make our expensive hardware choices obsolete. Should we move from CD-ROM to DVD? Should we skip all future software choices and migrate all our reference services online? There are compelling reasons to move electronic reference online. It is the least "messy" of all choices. CD-ROM towers are difficult to maintain. Online services require no technical support and they reach every Internet-connected classroom, regardless of platform or hardware. Online services meet users' expectations of currency by offering information that may be updated daily, even hourly. Through passwords and remote authentication, online services are conveniently accessible to students and community at home at any time of day as well as being a major public relations tool.

We are selecting software and resources in more formats than ever before, making far more expensive and expansive choices. In fact school librarians are or should now be making building, district, or community-wide decisions in creating "reference suites." But many of us are trying to squeeze print and CD-ROM and online resources into a budget that has been dormant for years. Central office must wake up and understand that something of value must run on the newly-installed network—that students need quality pay services in addition to their access to the uneven Web. This type of commitment is not a one-shot deal; it must be made annually.

School libraries are increasingly gathering together in groups to increase purchasing power. They are joining consortia, and consortia of consortia, often at the state level, to get the best possible deals on services to serve their larger communities. Public and academic libraries are joining school libraries to provide access to journal databases, encyclopedias, and curriculum resources. Libraries not providing state-of-the-art, online pay services do a disservice to their communities. They deprive many students of equitable access to high quality information and may leave students with the false impression that the Web will meet all their information needs.

There is excitement in the school online reference market, and service to students improves with every update. Vendors are providing an ever-increasing amount of full-text in their journal databases. Each of the major vendors now offers a service to meet the needs of the long-ignored intermediate and middle school populations. Vendors are recognizing the confusion that students experience with the increasing number of available interface choices. Databases are merging. Partnerships are forming. Most of the periodical vendors offer an encyclopedia as a free or an add-on service. UMI offers the option of including the ASCII text of the popular World Book Encyclopedia in its ProQuest Direct interface. KidQuest and JuniorQuest on the Web offer a topic tree browse and an attractive safari interface. Gale's merger with IAC as the Gale Group allows students to search the TOM journals databases and Gale's curricular reference in one step, using one comfortable interface. Using GaleNet's Web site, students can search across multiple databases, eliminating the need to use several individual CD-ROMs. A student looking for material on World War I might now find results leading her to Exploring Poetry and DISCovering Biography, as well as the world history product that might have been her first and only choice to check.

Many of the online reference services—EBSCO for instance—plan to incorporate quality Web pages into their search results. And our school vendors are also beginning to realize that student demand for information predates 1985. UMI is working on adding to the back end of its database so that students will begin to have full-text online journal access to the *Challenger* disaster, the Kent State student killings and, of course, Woodstock.

Our online catalogs are evolving too. Graphical interfaces invite young students to search. Maps of the library lead students easily to shelf locations. Curriculum Enhanced MARC offers additional fields for recording and locating materials that are more meaningful to school users. But if they are to be truly convenient, our catalogs must also migrate to the Web, following the example of university libraries. The Web provides an easy vehicle for the union catalog. Holdings are visible to the entire community from home or school, day or night. At a glance a student or parent at home will know which libraries in a school district, or a consortium, have the materials he or she needs. Having our holdings more visible to the larger community should inspire greater use of our collection, more efficient interlibrary loan, and students arriving prepared to seek materials. Pennsylvania's ACCESS-PA project is an example of a forward-thinking union catalog system, linking the catalogs of school, public, and academic libraries statewide (http://access pa.brodart.com/search/pz/pa.html).

PROFESSIONAL DEVELOPMENT

Without a guide, the Tin Man, the Lion, and the Scarecrow might not have ventured down the road. It is important to link arms with partners. No one wants to wander the woods alone. Mary Alice Anderson at Winona Middle School (Minnesota) is one librarian who is deeply involved in professional development of her faculty (see Figure 7.2). Anderson says:

> Staff development is a significant component of our school's media/technology program. We began with "how-tos" when our first lab was installed in 1986 and have continued as technology has improved and changed and curriculum integration has progressed. As the only media specialist in a 1,000-student school, I cannot possibly teach all of the students, but I can reach all of the teachers. Our initiatives include ongoing after-school classes that

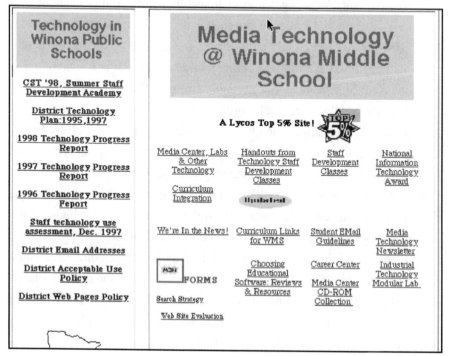

Figure 7.2

emphasize skills, half-day workshops intended to support curriculum integration, and a summer technology academy that is also open to teachers from other districts. We keep our help sheet rack well stocked and place many of our help sheets and staff development class materials on our Web site (http://wms.luminet.net/wmstechnology/ index.html) so they are accessible to our teachers and others at any time.

Anderson admits that staff development takes a lot of of her time, but considers the investment well spent as "teacher skills continue to increase, curriculum integration increases, and the "leading edge" teachers continue to move forward, bringing the others along."

Peter Milbury, librarian at Chico High School in California, is also a strong advocate of school librarians' involvement in faculty professional development:

I am thinking that the answer is in the space in between those who do and those who don't, and how we can narrow it. I see instructional development institutes, training, workshops, and seminars as a way to revitalize the role of the school librarian in the education community. There are many reasons why this approach is so effective: publicity, pride, enthusiasm, high profile—all of which reflect back on the school from the outside observer. Too many librarians are unable or unwilling to get into the instructional development role. However, I believe that is the most important role that we have, once the mechanical chores of running a library are taken care of.

LINKING ARMS WITH EACH OTHER

In the school library arena, professional development has been occurring online as well as off. Thanks to the Internet, we are no longer alone. The ICONnect task force (see Figure 7.3 on page 124) provides a wide variety of online courses for school librarians and teachers to update skills (http://www.ala. org/ICONN/ index.html).

School librarians have been sharing with colleagues for years through what may be the world's most powerful listserv. LM_NET (http://ericir.

Figure 7.3

syr.edu/lm_net), a discussion group created for school library media specialists which now boasts approximately 10,000 members, has connected the long-time unconnected. School librarians are among the most isolated professionals in the educational landscape. A social studies teacher or a third grade teacher has a team of colleagues with whom they can discuss ideas and problems. Public and academic librarians have librarian buddies within their facilities. In school libraries few of us have had that kind of faculty or break room support.

"People often write to me to express their thanks for LM_NET and the powerful help they receive as members," said Milbury, who is also one of the co-owners of LM_NET, when I asked him recently about the success of the list. "One of the most common themes I see is the variety of perspectives the LM_NET members receive from their postings to the group, along with the personal sense of camaraderie, and the fact that they are able to be in touch with other librarians without leaving their own schools and homes. One of the major benefits that LM_NET has been able to offer our profession is the ability to overcome the sense of professional isolation that many of us feel. This makes me feel very good about having been part of this remarkable group."

There is chat and professional chat. Recently LM_Chat and LM_Conf have brought a synchronous energy to professional dialog. Extending the success of LM_NET, a few school library pioneers have been experimenting with the viability of hosting real-time online meetings. LM_CHAT is a drop-in chat environment where, at any time of day, school librarians can login and participate in free-form synchronous conversation with colleagues. LM_CONF offers monthly virtual synchronous meetings for school librarians and features speakers, panelists, and organized discussions on topics of practical importance. The chats, which have focused on professional issues—from filters to orientation activities, to online reference products to intellectual freedom—are archived on the LM_NET page for those who cannot attend live sessions.

AND LINKING ARMS WITH OTHER FRIENDS

Traditionally vulnerable to budget cuts, school librarians have long understood the value of public relations and community involvement. The over-the-rainbow school library has an expanded view of community. School librarians have always linked themselves with their communities, inviting experts in to speak at special events and making use of generous parent volunteers. The Internet expands opportunities for collaboration and outreach, and school librarians are enhancing this connection, linking to the community with their Web pages and remote online services. Some often open their doors after school hours to deal with issues of equity or to provide evening technology workshops for adults. Online pay database services are increasingly offering access to quality information after school and increasing the awareness of the type of service a school library can offer.

I have grown to view reference in a larger sense. Reference questions from students often pop into my e-mail. They range from how to cite an unusual source, to recommending a good summer read, to where to go for guidance with a personal problem. Participation in the American Association of School Librarian's KidsConnect service (http://www.ala. org/ICONN/kidsconn. html) has allowed many of us to use our reference skills in a global setting. Through the KidsConnect project, school librarians from around the world offer quality reference services to students worldwide via e-mail. As an initiative of ICONnect project, KidsConnect is evidence of the strong presence and contribution being made by school librarians as information specialists on the Internet.

Community connections can go both ways. The Internet makes it easier to mine local talent. I am currently creating an accessible database of experts—community members with special areas of knowledge who will make themselves available as e-mail mentors. These experts may include a World War II veteran, an origami artist, a chemist, a patent attorney, or a professional Web page designer.

CREATING THE YELLOW BRICK ROAD; OR THERE'S NO PLACE LIKE HOME (PAGE)

Many of our school libraries now have two front doors. The effective school library Web page pulls together, in one unified interface, all of a library's resources—print and electronic. It offers guidance while it fosters independent learning. It models careful selection. And, it also redefines community. The best examples of these have become popular beyond their schools and their communities, making a major contribution to reference, readers' advisory, and collection development on the Web. They point strongly to the tremendous real and potential contribution of librarians.

I sincerely believe the very best instructional tool I have ever created has been my library Web page (http://mciunix.mciu.k12.pa.us/~whslib). Though it is certainly not the very best example of a school library Web page, it represents the curriculum of my school, and makes our students' vast array of information choices manageable (see Figure 7.4). My Web page represents the school library to the school community and the outside world. It is my starting point for instruction, the point from which I demonstrate and guide students in searching, location, and evaluation skills. The Web page functions as a visual representation of reference, guidance, and collection development. Inclusion of a link on the Web page is equivalent to selection of a book or a video. I select sites I find appropriate to our curriculum: those that will enhance the learning experiences of my students and further the research needs of my students at their various levels of experience.

Figure 7.4

A school library Web page does not have to be fancy; it has to be functional. As a teacher and librarian, I want students to visit sites I consider valuable. The first screen that my students see should offer them a guide to the resources I think will help them the most. I want them to have quicker access to materials related to the curricula of their teachers. Bookmarking worked for a while, but it was an impractical solution because I had to continually update fifty un-networked workstations. Bookmarks could not follow the students to their home desktops.

But just as a school library provides more than just books, a school library Web page provides more than just links to Web sites. I have attempted to provide the equivalent of electronic reference by including my search tips, bibliographic style sheets, and the other really cool handouts that students never seem to be able to hold on to in paper form. For summer vacation use, I plan to post faculty summer reading lists.

There is no one right way to create a library Web page. The panoply of options is available to view, through links generously gathered by Peter Milbury, Chico, California (http://www.cusd.chico.k12.ca.us/~pmilbury/lib. html) and Linda Bertland of Stetson Middle School, Philadelphia (http://www.voicenet.com/~bertland/libs.html). On his Best of the Web Outstanding School Libraries and Media Centers (http://w3.trib.com/~rmhs/

library/best.html), John M. Bernhisel, librarian at Rocky Mountain High School in Byron, Wyoming, posts his picks for excellence in this arena. Milbury himself has selected and identified a select group that represents best practice (see Figure 7.5).

Debbie Abilock (Hillsborough, California) is among the many school library Web pioneers. Her page is recognized widely, and not just by librarians. The strength of Abilock's Nueva School Research Page is her content (see Figure 7.6), which is a model of research strategies and tips (http://www.nueva.pvt. k12.ca.us/~debbie/library/research/research.html).

Kathy Schrock, formerly a librarian and currently a technology coordinator, has set the model for collection of reference links, instruction in evaluation, and the sharing of staff development resources. Her Web page (http://www.capecod.net/schrockguide/) is used by educators worldwide.

I can hear the whining from many corners. Suggesting that school librarians add the job of Webmaster to the towering list of duties already performed with limited support may seem unreasonable. And yet, if we want to offer complete service, if we want to serve the entire school community, if we truly want to expand our influence, we must think about access and service in much larger ways.

Why should a school librarian maintain a Web page? The school library Web page offers these benefits:

- It is open twenty-four hours, seven days a week, on demand and at the point of need. With its larger public to serve, the public library cannot meet the specific needs of K-12 students. However, public and school librarians can collaborate in many ways. School library handouts (the MLA style sheet, for instance) and sites selected to support class assignments are made easier to locate for the public librarian as well as the student who needs them at midnight.
- It is a significant public relations tool. Parents may never read the library newsletter but will understand a new concept of library service when they see their children using the library Web page to help them complete their assignments.
- It represents a library's philosophy. Many school library Web pages express the mission of the library to the public.
- It provides services needed by students. School library Web pages guide high school students in their search for college and careers,

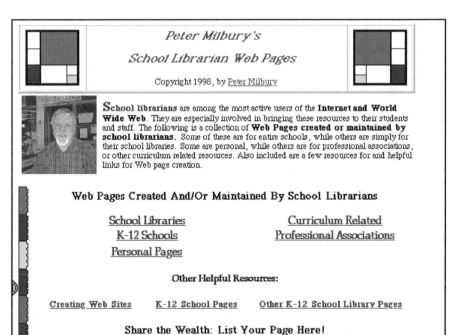

Figure 7.5

Figure 7.6

offer sites related to their recreational needs, and provide links to resources for specific assignments.

- It offers professional development materials for teachers, linking teachers to lesson plans, standards, and readings about educational trends and effective pedagogy.
- It offers a visible place to post policy. Students should have easy access to their library's circulation, copyright, procedural and acceptable use policies, as well as any guidelines for creating Web pages to be stored on the school's server.
- It models selection. The criteria used in selecting more tangible materials are now employed in selecting links for the school library Web page. The librarian's choice endorses quality, as the online translation of collection building.
- It offers instruction and guidance. Many school library Web pages host tutorials on Internet searching and evaluation of materials. This is a perfect place to point students to subject directories and search engines and to post the district's style sheet and evaluation tools.
- It offers remote reference service in a variety of ways: links to the excellent reference areas and links to online pay services—encyclopedias, journal indexes, and reprint services. An e-mail link to KidsConnect, or the address of an "ask an expert page," offers students access to quality guidance from their homes. The librarian may also elect to include his or her own e-mail address.
- It links students to other resources within the community. This is an effective way to expose students to the collections of local public, special, and academic libraries as well as the resources of nearby museums and historical societies.
- It offers a place to store those local treasures that previously went completely unrecognized—school and community histories, student-collected oral histories, and photographs.
- It can inspire off-line reading with the inclusion of hot picks, student reviews (interactive!), new additions, curricular and summer reading lists, and award-winning book lists.
- It offers a place for students to publish. The school library page can host the school newspaper as well as examples of written and multimedia projects.

There are other school personnel preparing Web pages, but the school librarian is the staff member best qualified to pull together the information resources of the school. Jamie McKenzie, educational technology consultant and editor of the ejournal *From Now On*, notes,

> As many schools are venturing into Web publishing, it seems to me that the best person to coordinate development of the school's Web site is the library media specialist. This is because the Web site is actually an information system, and library media folks are the information specialists, the infotects, if you will, who should help to coordinate the design of information delivery systems. In all too many districts, the design of networks and Web sites is handled by those with strong technology backgrounds and skills but little classroom experience or awareness of information literacy issues. Library media specialists can make sure that school Web sites provide much more than PR, sports news, and fancy moving GIFs.

Frances Jacobson, librarian at the University Laboratory High School in Urbana Illinois (http://www.uni.uiuc.edu/library), describes school library Web pages "as becoming de facto front ends to our information sources. They will be the single gateway to the library's catalog, periodical databases, the Web, Usenet, local information, school archives, and all manner of electronic information. In the hands of the school library media specialist, these Web pages are more likely to be cohesive, user friendly, and pedagogically sound. They will also be interactive—a place to discuss books (or whatever), collaboratively build information referral points, and ask reference questions."

LIONS AND TIGERS AND BEARS

The road ahead is not perfectly clear. When it is suggested that the school library can be easily replaced by the Internet, we must be sure our own vision is clear. Evolving roles and new positions created by technology have created fuzzy borders. The good witches no longer stay in the North and South, and the bad witches no longer stay in the East and West. We are carving out our new roles with new colleagues. In the best of all possible worlds, school librarians will carve out a niche as very good witches, the information technology specialists in a school or district, collaborating with classroom teachers and technology teachers to integrate information skills and deliver quality resources. But new connections with network administrators and technology coordinators may create turf issues. Who selects which software? Who troubleshoots? Who delivers technology inservicing? Who demonstrates PowerPoint? And, perhaps, the most important question is who owns the budget for technology? While the technology coordinator, with input from all faculty, might select the productivity suite to be resident on the school's network, it is the librarian who should be responsible for selecting the electronic reference suite. There are colleagues of mine who have not yet carved for themselves a role in the school culture as information technology specialists. They are abdicating a great deal of power and losing an opportunity to set a direction for children. Will their rightful roles be absorbed by the technology teachers or directors?

We are torn in our instincts and loyalties. Defending intellectual freedom was far easier before the networks arrived. Districts are worried about litigation and parents are worried about the influence of the "inappropriate." Many of us are compromising our long held ideals and coping in a filtered environment.

My vision of the future of school libraries is not shared universally. There are colleagues who are struggling in facilities with no budgets, no resources, and no administrative support. There are many who struggle without support staff to process and shelve and file. How can they focus their efforts on a strong student-centered program? Where there may be new monies available for technology, many librarians now struggle to maintain any print collection at all.

Many teachers still see school librarians in a support rather than a leadership role. They have not yet seen the roads we can create. They view us as curators rather than consultants and partners in the learning process.

THE NEED TO LEARN TO USE YOUR GIFTS

"A library is a growing organism," wrote S. R. Ranganathan in *The Five Laws of Library Science* (1931). That statement has never been more true. It is now one of those organisms that is not confined by time and space. With pedagogy changing and information technologies evolving, it is hard to know what to learn or do first. School librarians are caught in a whirlwind of change and are now at a critical turning point.

Our new standards can help define us. *Information Power: Building Partnerships for Learning* (1998), and its companion document *Information Literacy for Student Learning* (1998), clearly delineate the emerging role of the library and the library information specialist in the school program. They describe the connections between information literacy, curricular content, and learning. They offer a guidebook for our explorations and a road plan to share with administrators, faculty, and parents. This is unmapped turf. It is up to school librarians to make it work—to interpret information skills for the rest of the school community and to ensure they are achieved, while recognizing the need for ethical behavior in a digital environment. We can carve out vital roles for ourselves and for our colleagues in other areas of the library world.

Our students are packed and ready to go. It is up to us to create roads. Where should these roads lead? Every little yellow brick should take our students and our communities down the road to information literacy. Unlike Dorothy's, our road is not already in place. We are piecing it together as we explore and build on our own talents, learning about the glittering lights of Oz and integrating the old-fashioned wisdom that has always served us well.

To a large degree, we are better than wizards. We offer gifts that will last a lifetime. We help people learn to solve problems using information. Virtual libraries will grow increasingly important, but strong school library programs are not about technology; they are about human interaction with information.

References

Anderson, M.A. (maryalic@wms.luminet.net). (1998, August 16). Qoutes. E-mail to J. Valenza (jvalenza @mciunix.mciu.k12.pa.us).

Craver, K. W. (1994). *School library media centers in the 21st century*. Westport, CT: Greenwood Press.

Information literacy standards for student learning (1998). Chicago: American Library Association.

Information power: Building partnerships for learning (1998). Chicago: American Library Association.

Jacobson, F.F. (francey@uiuc.edu). (1998, July 13). Qoute. E-mail to J. Valenza (jvalenza@mciunix. mciu.k12.pa.us).

Johnson, D. (1997). *The indispensible librarian: Surviving (and thriving) in school media centers in the information age*. Worthington, OH: Linworth Publishing.

Joseph, L. C. (1999). *Net curriculum: An educator's guide to using the Internet*. Medford, NJ: CyberAge Books/Information Today.

McKenzie, J. (mckenzie@fno.org). (1998, July 26). Permission. E-mail to J. Valenza (jvalenza@ mciunix.mciu.k12.pa.us).

McKenzie, J. (mckenzie@fno.org). *From now on: The information technology journal.* (http://fromnowon.org).

Milbury, P. (pmilbury@cusd.chico.k12.ca.us). (1998, July 30). Qoute. E-mail to J. Valenza (jvalenza@mciunix.mciu.k12.pa.us).

Ranganathan, S. R. (1931). *Five laws of library science.* Madras: Madras Library Association.

Recommended Resources

Crawford, W. & Gorman, M. (1995). Future libraries: Dreams and madness. Chicago: American Library Association.

Joseph, L. C. (1995). *World link: An Internet guide for educators, parents and students.* Columbus, OH: Greyden Press.

LeBaron, J. F., Collier, C. & de Lyon Friel, L. (1997). *A travel agent in cyber school: The Internet and the library media program.* Englewood, CO: Libraries Unlimited.

Extending the Library to Remote Learners:
Critical Issues and Current Initiatives

Vicky York
Associate Professor and Distance Education Coordinator
Montana State University Libraries
Bozeman, Montana

INTRODUCTION

The convergence of several trends over the past few years mandate that librarians and distance learning providers focus their attention on meeting the library needs of remote learners. These trends include the tremendous growth of distance learning programs, the emergence of the World Wide Web as an instructional and informational format, and the increasing recognition of the importance of electronic library skills. Not only in North America, but also worldwide, higher education is facing a dramatic paradigm shift. A recent discussion paper, *Information Resources and Library Services for Distance Learners: A Framework for Quality*, from the Consortium for Educational Technology for University Systems (CETUS) characterized the transformed university as "one more student-centered, less place dependent, and significantly enabled by technology" (1997, p. 3).

News stories, like the announcement by the Western Governors University that it had entered into an agreement with the China Internet Education Center to collaborate on the development and delivery of distance learning programs, or the one by the Zambian government that one million Zambians have applied for the distance education program that was introduced last year, dramatize the potential of delivering educational programs globally. Although many scholars have voiced concerns about the academic quality of electronically delivered distance education programs, all indicators point to continued growth in the number of students enrolled in these programs.

JUSTIFICATION FOR LIBRARY INVOLVEMENT

Library services must be an integral part of any distance learning program. *A Guide for Planning Library Integration into Distance Education Programs* states that "library services are not just another support service; they are a necessary component of any educational experience and an integral component of a lifelong learning process" (York, 1993, p. 1). It is clear that the same technologies that have opened new doors for distance education have, at the same time, raised new challenges for libraries. Two of the most critical areas demanding our attention are the costs for electronic services and publications and the mechanisms for providing those students enrolled in distance programs with equitable access to library resources. Fortunately, there are encouraging signs that rather than reacting at the eleventh hour, many libraries are fully engaged in the dialogues taking place on their campuses and in their communities and are becoming valued partners in these discussions.

Libraries have been providing services to nontraditional students for decades. In the broadest sense, it can be argued that public libraries were far ahead of their academic counterparts in the late nineteenth and early twentieth centuries in meeting the educational needs of the many newly arrived immigrants and others seeking educational opportunities. However, as more institutions of higher education began offering formal off-campus programs in the second half of this century, the Association of College and Research Libraries acknowledged the role academic libraries play when it issued its original *Guidelines for Extended Campus Library Services* in 1981. In 1996, the Association of Research Libraries surveyed its 119 members to determine the extent of library involvement in distance education activities; to determine what kinds of library services were being delivered to remote patrons; and to ascertain how these services were being managed. Of the 74 (62 percent) of the libraries that responded, two thirds indicated that they participated at some level in providing library services to students and faculty involved in distance

education programs. The types and management of these services vary widely. Traditionally, they have included access to the library's online catalog, e-
mail and/or phone-in reference service (often via a toll-free number), delivery
by mail and/or fax of books and copies of journal articles, site collections,
electronic reserves, and bibliographic instruction. Responsibility for coordinating and managing library services also varies. It may be more narrowly
incorporated into an area like library instruction or a broader area like outreach. One trend is to have a designated person serving as off-campus services librarian or coordinator.

Opportunities for involvement in distance education will only increase,
and library administrators must think through the implications for their
organizations. Whatever approach the library takes, there is a wide range of
components that must come together with the technology to make a successful distance program. Other departments outside the library manage
many of these components, so it is important that the library be a player.

GUIDELINES AND STANDARDS

The academic library community's recognition of these opportunities,
as well as the information needs created by the growth of distance learning programs, is evidenced by the new revision of the 1990 ACRL guidelines, published in 1998 in *College & Research Libraries News*. As
explained in the Introduction, the decision to revise the 1990 guidelines
was based on the growth of nontraditional educational opportunities, and
"the decrease in central campus enrollments, the search for more cost-
effective sources for post-secondary education, and the appearance and
rapid development of the virtual or all-electronic university, having no
physical campus of its own" (p. 689). A major shift has been to emphasize the responsibility of the parent institution to set overall direction and
provide the funding to meet the library's expanded role. Even the new
title, *ACRL Guidelines for Distance Learning Library Services*, reflects
the articulation of a broader scope and the growing importance that
"library resources and services in institutions of higher education must
meet the needs of all their faculty, students, and academic support staff,
wherever these individuals are located, whether on main campuses, off
campus, in distance education or extended campus programs, or in the
absence of a campus at all; in courses taken for credit or non-credit; in

continuing education programs; in courses attended in person or by means of electronic transmission; or any other means of distanced education" (p. 689).

At the same time that libraries see themselves playing a larger role in providing services for remote learners, they also see increasing costs, tighter budgets, and higher expectations of library users. The Canadian Library Association, also tackling a revision of their *Guidelines for Library Support of Distance and Distributed Learning in Canada* (1998), acknowledges the pressures of rising costs and cutbacks and the "danger that inconsistencies in library support for Canadian distance learning programs will be increased as smaller institutions struggle to even maintain on-campus service." An article appearing in *the NODE: networking*, an online publication of *USA Today*, observed that "technology may well be putting distance learners at an even greater disadvantage by creating a still more uneven playing field than before" (1998, p. 1).

Many students who take courses away from campus rely on their local school or public library. A survey for a class project at the Emporia State University's School of Library and Information Management (SLIM) showed that distance students relied on a variety of libraries for their research needs. Of the twenty SLIM respondents, ten indicated that they relied primarily on another library, including public, school, and other academic libraries, the state library, and a law library (Halverson, 1998).

Many branch campus or smaller academic libraries are ill-prepared to support the distance courses offered by their main campuses or other institutions. An article that appeared, interestingly enough, in the "Inside Politics" column of the *Salt Lake City Weekly* raised the issue of who pays when students of online education programs descend on their public libraries for help (Biele, 1998, p. 1). With guidelines and principles for resources and service being set in place, libraries of all sizes and types are now having to confront the economic realities of the information marketplace and funding priorities of their parent institutions or political jurisdictions.

Concerns about promoting the need for library services to off-campus learners and raising the issues surrounding equitable services have begun to enter the mainstream of library consciousness. Until a few years ago, articles and research about library services to remote learners appeared infrequently in the standard library journals. In 1982, a forward-looking group from Central Michigan State University organized the first Off-Campus Library Services

Conference. Since then, this conference has provided a forum to share ideas, research, and new perspectives. The published conference papers have helped to form a growing body of literature in the field of library services to remote learners. In fact, *Library Services for Off-Campus and Distance Education: The Second Annotated Bibliography* (Slade & Kascus, 1996) identifies over 500 recent sources of information.

Current news and developments can be gleaned through the listservs OFF-CAMP (OFFCAMP@lists.wayne.edu) and DISTLIB (listserv@lib.lake-headu.ca). In response to the growing interest in library services for remote learners, a new peer-reviewed electronic publication, *The Journal of Library Services for Distance Education* (*JLSDE*) (www.westga.edu/library/jlsde/) debuted in August 1997. The brainchild of editor Carol Goodson, *JLSDE*, makes a substantial contribution towards filling the gap for information in this developing field. The Canadian Library Association's Library Services for Distance Learning Interest Group's newsletter, *Distlib Digest,* has also recently become available in an electronic form.

With the advent of the World Wide Web, and the understandable temptation of students to see it as a big library, the need to teach students to critically evaluate electronic sources seems to have taken some educators by surprise. It has been interesting to see library resources and information literacy issues appearing more frequently in the postings of nonlibrary, academic listservs like DEOS-L: The Distance Education Online Symposium (DEOS-L@lists.psu.edu) and the American Association of Higher Education's AAH-ESGIT (aahesgit@list.cren.net). While approaches differ, respondents (including library directors) all stress that there must be an articulation of institutional responsibility for helping students achieve "information literacy," and they consider librarians to be the most capable of playing this role.

One result of the maturation of distance education as a field is that the library issues are being addressed more often in the distance education literature. The growing recognition of some of the common interests between librarians and distance educators is reflected in the book, *The Distance Learner's Guide*, edited by Dr. George Connick (1998), President Emeritus of the Education Network of Maine. Along with chapters on choosing a distance education provider, the role of the computer, and career planning, Connick has included "The Distant Learner's Library: The Indispensable Guide to Finding the Material." Necessarily general in description, it provides some very good advice on finding and using both traditional and online library services, along with the admonition to make the librarian the distance learner's best friend. Basic guidance, such as this, for distance education students, points up the opportunity for continued study by librarians of the needs and information-seeking patterns of remote users. Distance education providers and librarians still have much to learn from each other.

The partnership between librarians and distance education providers is only one of the relationships which must be developed. Collaboration among all the stakeholders is crucial to successfully providing library services. Substantial planning, partnering, and policy evaluation needs to occur if library services and resources are to be fully integrated into a distance learning program. No library, particularly an academic library, operates in a vacuum. The growing recognition and understanding that many of the decisions related to providing electronic information and the concomitant library skills must be made at the institution, system, and state level have greatly expanded the dialogue among university administrators, librarians, distance educators, and computing professionals.

The Consortium for Educational Technology for University Systems (CETUS), whose library services report was mentioned earlier, had its genesis in a committee formed in 1994 by the chief executives of higher education of systems in America's two largest states, California and New York. Eventually, a diverse range of participants was brought together to design the framework, which included library services. Similarly, the revised ACRL guidelines received review and input from many educational organizations, including CETUS, various accrediting associations, the Western Cooperative for Educational Telecommunications (WCET), and the Canadian Library Association.

MODEL PROGRAMS

One of the hallmarks of those most successful in providing library services is the wide range of collaboration and cooperation among those involved. There are currently many examples of good practices, but three initiatives stand out. These go beyond models of library service by serving as demonstrations of leadership in distance education with strong state or provincial and institutional commitment to educational telecommunications, innovative use of information technologies, and close, ongoing relationships among the various stakeholders.

As a state, Florida has made a substantial investment in distance learning. In 1996, the Florida legislature funded the Florida Public Postsecondary Institute on Distance Learning, an organization created by the Community College and State University Systems to coordinate the development of the distance learning program and infrastructure. A look at Florida's Campus (http://www.flcampus.org) shows some 1,300 distance learning courses from which students can choose. The library component is no less ambitious. The Florida Distance Learning Library Initiative (http://www.dos.state.fl.us/dlli/) is a cooperative effort of the Community College System, the State University System, and the public libraries of Florida through collaboration with the State Library of Florida. Its purpose is simple and clear: to provide cost-effective, expanded access to library services in support of distance learning. This support includes five initial components: electronic resources, reference and referral services, library user training, borrowing privileges and document delivery. Describing this prototype project, Dr. Tracey Burdick is optimistic that the "vision will become reality over the next five years," in large part because "through this initiative Florida has begun a systematic, planned, multi-faceted approach that builds on the existing strengths and cooperation of Florida's libraries" (1998, p. 4).

In Canada, British Columbia's Open Learning Agency (http://www.ola.bc.ca) offers a model of collaboration at the provincial level. Among the goals of the Ministry of Advanced Education and Job Training's 1989 "Access for All" educational strategy were those of expanding open learning opportunities and fostering innovation through the use of new technologies. Libraries were recognized as an integral part of the "Access for All" vision, giving rise to the Electronic Library Network (http://www.ola.bc.ca/eln), a cooperative of twenty-nine participating libraries across the province. The Electronic Library Network provides British Columbia union databases, indexing and abstracting databases, Internet training manuals, library skills modules, and document delivery services. Perhaps most importantly, it has developed a model for resource sharing that minimizes duplication and overall costs for the partner libraries.

The initiative with which I am personally most familiar is the Western Governors University (WGU). In 1995, the Western Governors' Association agreed to collaborate in the development and delivery of distance learning courses and programs. Initially proposed by the governors of Utah and Colorado, seventeen states have now signed on. From the beginning, an active group of librarians sought to keep library issues in front of the designers, who in turn solicited input and involvement from the larger library community. In addition to course and degree offerings, the WGU consciously planned for library services. Made up of representatives from the pilot institutions, a working group was established to put specific building blocks in place. To this end, WGU solicited requests for proposals for bookstore, registration, library services, and other essential services in spring 1997. As indicated in the RFP for the Central Library Resource, "a premise of the Western Governors University is that the quality of library service available to distant students must be essentially the same as that provided to on-campus students." The University of New Mexico General Library was selected as the Central Library Resource provider and has put into place four basic components: (1) a Web page with links to resources, services, instruction guides, and the provider institutions' online library catalogs; (2) online access to full-text and citation databases; (3) reference, document delivery, interlibrary loan, and technical assistance; and (4) Internet service accounts. The Central Library Resource is positioned to grow and develop as the course and program offerings begin to go online over the next few years.

ACCESS TO DIGITAL CONTENT

These examples, as well as many others, demonstrate that there are ways to share costs for online services and electronic publications and provide the mechanisms to allow access to students enrolled in distance programs. New models of publishing are beginning to emerge. Projects such as JSTOR (http://www.jstor.org) and the Johns Hopkins University's MUSE (http://www. press.jhu.edu/muse.html) are addressing the need to build an electronic collection of scholarly journals through cost sharing among many libraries. They are successfully demonstrating that publishers, scholarly associations, and libraries can work together with a broader vision. As the examples of the Florida Distance Learning Initiative, the Electronic Library Network, and the Western Governors University show, there is strength in numbers. Library consortia are able to negotiate license agreements with publishers and database vendors at costs that would be prohibitive for individual members. At the same time, students are provided with access to a greater variety of indexes and full-text products. But these partnerships do not come about without substantial planning, program evaluation, and recognition of the conflicting needs of the participants. To help libraries tackle these kinds of issues, The International Coalition of Library Consortia (ICOLC) has prepared a statement on "Current Perspective and Preferred Practices for the Selection and Purchase of Electronic Information." The statement is "intended to provide a starting point for dialogue among information providers and library consortia," and offers practices for the pricing and delivery of electronic scholarly information (see http://www.ola.bc.ca/eln/pands/endorsement/htm).

ASSESSMENT

The premise that the quality of library service to off-campus students equals that provided to on-campus students underlies all the initiatives mentioned in this chapter. As has already been pointed out, many public and local libraries are not prepared to meet the needs of postsecondary education distance learners. Some students simply live too far away from any physical library. Providing equitable access requires another set of collaborative relationships, usually among the educational institution's own organizational entities and the state's higher education system. Not only the library, but the registrar's office, computing center, and the departments offering the courses are among the stakeholders whose input must be solicited in the planning process. Again the technology offers both potential and problems. How do you provide the online resources to legitimate students of a distance education program and abide by licensing and copyright restrictions without restricting access? The technology now allows for more sophisticated authorization systems such as personal identification (PIN) or student numbers. These systems are expensive, however, and many university computing centers are only starting to bring them online. Nonetheless, as time and place no longer define enrollments, it is imperative that barriers be removed if equitable access to online materials is to be assured. In the Florida, British Columbia, and Western Governors University examples, authentication for student access has been built into the overall program.

Some argue that library services for distance learners have not kept pace with the growing number of distance education programs. Most people involved in distance learning acknowledge that we are entering into a brave new world where the old models no longer apply. As often happens, the technology has outpaced the response of most educational institutions to change the way they approach teaching, learning, and knowledge creation. The Internet has done a great deal to decrease the time it takes to find some kinds of information, but little to increase the availability of scholarly materials. Moreover, access to those materials that are available electronically is often limited to computers physically in the library or the campus network. Rather than building the "library without walls," we are erecting higher and thicker walls for those learners not on campus.

It must be clear by now that we are all in this together. If the promise of technology for library services to remote learners is to be fully realized, collaborative relationships must be sought out and developed on many levels. There is no reason that we as librarians should not be the ones to initiate that process.

References

Biele, K. (1998, July 16). Virtual sticking point. *Salt Lake City Weekly*, p. 1. (http://www.slweekly.com/news/politics/politics_980716.html)

Burdick, T. (1998, June). One state's approach: The Florida distance learning library initiative. *Journal of Library Services for Distance Education*, 1 (2), 4. (http://www.westga.edu/library/jlsde/)

Connick, G. (Ed.) (1998). *Distance learner's guide*. New York: Prentice-Hall.

Consortium for Educational Technology for University Systems (1997). *Information resources and library services for distance learners: A framework for quality*. Seal Beach, CA: The Trustees of California State University.

Guidelines for distance learning library services. (1998, October). *College & Research Libraries News, 59*, 689-694.

Halverson, R. (1998, Spring). *Perceived quality of information resource access for School of Library and Information Management students of Emporia State University*, p. 3. (unpublished survey conducted for LI830).

Library Services for Distance Learning Interest Group, Canadian Library Association. (1998). Draft guidelines. (http://uviclib.uvic.ca/staff/sslade/guidelines.html)

Library Services for Distance Learners. (1998, June). *the NODE: networking* (http://node.on.ca/networking/june1998/)

Slade, A. & Kascus, M. (1996). *Library services to off-campus and distance education: The second annotated bibliography*. Boulder: Libraries Unlimited.

York, V. (1993). *A guide for planning library integration into distance education programs*. Boulder, CO: Western Interstate Commission for Educational Telecommunications. (http://www.wiche.edu)

Recommended Resources

Lee, T. & Jenda, C. (1998). *The role of ARL libraries in extension/outreach*. SPEC Kit 233. Washington, DC: Association of Research Libraries.

Snyder, C., Logue, S. & Preece, B. (1996). *Role of libraries in distance education*. SPEC Kit 216. Washington, DC: Association of Research Libraries.

Understanding Networks and Telecommunications Infrastructure

George Machovec
Technical Director
Colorado Alliance of Research Libraries
Denver, Colorado

Telecommunications and networking play a central role in the evolving virtual library. The network is the centerpiece that links servers and end users. Without the network there is no virtual library. The computer world is changing daily as companies come and go, new products are introduced (and last year's products become antiquated), new standards are developed, and new terms are introduced. The networking world is very complex and evolving rapidly. This chapter will provide an overview of some of the basic terminology and trends which librarians will encounter as they continue to expand in the digital world. As huge bodies of literature are available on virtually every topic mentioned in this chapter, this presentation is meant merely as a brief primer to a few key topics.

WHAT IS A COMPUTER NETWORK?

In the beginning was the mainframe computer. All connections to this central device were made through input/output devices such as "dumb" terminals, printers, card readers, magnetic tape, and other devices; computer jobs were run in batch, and there was almost no direct interaction with the computer. Since the invention of the computer, one of the most important improvements has been the development of the network: computers and devices linked together through telecommunications so that they could communicate with each other.

Since the late 1970s, computer systems have changed from a centralized to a distributed architecture. Computer networks have also continued to evolve through a linking of computers and users by providing paths between systems at local, regional, and international levels. Internetworking between dissimilar devices on heterogeneous networks has allowed users to communicate on a growing scale. TCP/IP (Transmission Control Protocol/Internet Protocol) has become the most common internetworking protocol linking computers and users around the world through the Internet.

Computer networks are also migrating from analog to digital circuits. Nearly all modern high-speed networks are digital in nature. A notable exception is that many of the voice grade telephone lines that come into homes are still analog, requiring that modems be used with personal computers for linking to the outside world. This is changing, however, as phone service providers and others rush to install in homes high-speed digital connections such as ISDN (integrated services digital network), fiber optics, cable connections to the Internet, and ADSL (asymmetric digital subscriber lines).

LIBRARIES NEED TO PLAN FOR CHANGE

With the rapidly evolving nature of computing and networks, libraries must plan for change. Unlike traditional printed materials which remain virtually unchanged over time (with the exception of aging, wear and tear), computers and their networks must be replaced and upgraded on a relatively frequent basis. These key factors are forcing this change:

- Hardware and networking infrastructure are quickly changing.
- Commercial carriers are offering a wide array of transport services and speeds which are constantly improving (e.g., digital leased lines, frame relay, ISDN, ATM).
- Library and end-user bandwidth needs are quickly rising as more complex information and multimedia is distributed over the Internet.

It is imperative that libraries work closely with their parent organization or funding agencies to convince decision-makers of library needs and upgrading requirements.

BANDWIDTH

One of the key issues in any network is bandwidth. Bandwidth defines the transmission capacity of a communications channel. Local needs and available funding usually have the greatest influence on how much bandwidth can be acquired. The general consensus is that more is better. Building infrastructure, the kind of wiring, and other network hardware in a building or an organization will also play a key role. Typical bandwidth terminology includes:

- 56Kbps: a data transmission speed of 56,000 bits per second.
- T1: a data transmission speed of 1.544 Mbps (1.544 million bits per second). Also referred to as DS1 (digital signal 1).
- Fractional T1: some subset of a T1 line usually defined by some number of 64 Kbps channels.
- T3: a transmission speed of 44 Mbps (44 million bits per second). Also referred to as DS3 (digital signal level 3).
- Ethernet LANS (local area networks): operate at speeds of 10 Mbps.
- Fast Ethernet LANs: operate at speeds of 100 Mbps.
- OC1 (optical carrier 1): 51.84 Mbps—Also referred to as STS1 (synchronous transport signal level 1).
- OC3 (optical carrier 3): 155.52 Mbps—Also referred to as STS3.
- OC 12 (optical carrier 12): 622.080 Mbps—Also referred to as STS12.
- OC24 (optical carrier 24): 1244.160 Mbps—Also referred to as STS24.
- Gigabit network: a general term usually used to describe networks operating at 1 Gbps (gigabit per second) or faster.

LOCAL AREA NETWORKS AND LAN INTERNETWORKING

A local area network (LAN) is a cluster of interconnected PCs, servers, and other devices in a relatively small area (e.g., a building). LANs connect heterogeneous devices and allow such services as printing, file sharing, e-mail, CD-ROM access, gateways to the Internet or Intranets, and access to organizational computing (e.g., integrated library system or mainframe).

LANs primarily use one of three topologies:

- Bus topology: all devices are attached to a single cable running between two points, and all nodes receive the message through the cable at the same time.
- Star topology: a central device (hub) has all other devices in the network linked to it.
- Ring topology: a network in a closed loop with each node in the network connected to the next. Messages move only in one direction unless a dual loop is used.

Local area networks use two major transmission techniques: CSMA/CD (carrier sense multiple access with collision detection) or token passing. In a CSMA/CD LAN, data are being sent by one node; then if it detects a collision with other data, the node waits and retransmits. This is the technique used in Ethernet networks. Token passing networks use an electronic "token" which is passed around a network, allowing only the station at a time to transmit or receive.

Ethernet (and its cousin "Fast Ethernet") is the most common LAN networking technology in use today. It was originally developed by Xerox in 1976 and usually operates at speeds of 10Mbps or 100Mbps. It uses the CSMA/CD transmission technique and data may be carried over a variety of physical media such as twisted pair wiring, coax cable, fiber optics, or even wireless. Most Ethernet networks are designed with the bus topology.

FDDI (fiber distributed data interface) is another high speed LAN technology often used as an institutional backbone over which LANs connect. It uses fiber optics and often employs a dual token ring design for high speed redundant service. CDDI (copper distributed data interfaces) is another high speed (greater than 100 Mbps) networking technology which operates over copper twisted pair wiring and can be interfaced with FDDI backbones.

Some other older but still used LAN transmission techniques include LocalTalk which uses shielded twisted pair wiring and connectors from Apple Computer for linking Macintosh and other devices in an AppleTalk network. IBM token ring networks are an older technology from IBM that uses token passing in a ring topology.

LINKING LANS AND OTHER HARDWARE

A huge array of hardware and software is required to make networks operate both internally and between each other (internetworking). Some of the most common pieces of hardware are listed here:

- Network Interface Card (NIC): An expansion board for a PC, server or printer which connects to network cabling (e.g., twisted pair, coax) and supports the protocol required by the LAN (e.g., Ethernet).
- Repeater: A device which boosts electrical signals to increase transmission distance.
- Bridge: A hardware device used to link LANs to exchange data. Bridges can work with LANs with different wiring or network protocols.
- Router: An intelligent device that can send data packets to the correct network address and is protocol dependent using a hierarchical address of that protocol. Routers can support security, protocol translations, network management, etc.
- Hubs: Devices that retransmit data signals, allowing the network to be extended to multiple workstations or servers. In some star networks a hub may be the central controlling device. Hubs may be managed or unmanaged. Fast hubs operate in 100 Mbps networks.
- Multiplexers (or mux): A device that merges several lower-speed transmission channels into one high-speed channel at one end of a link with another mux to reverse the process on the other side. This can be accomplished by frequency division, time division, or statistical multiplexing.
- CSU/DSU (Channel Service Unit/Data Service Unit): A device that is used with digital data circuits to terminate a line and act as a buffer between the customer's equipment and a wide area network. It functions like a "modem" in an analog circuit.
- Gateway: A device connecting between two dissimilar networks that adds security, flow control, and protocol conversion. It can also be a shared connection between a LAN and a larger network. Gateways are slower than a bridge or router and include hardware and software. This term is also used to talk about passing from one online system to another (e.g., OPAC to OCLC).

- Switches: Similar to bridges but with more ports. Each of these ports may be dedicated to a segment of a network or individual devices such as servers, workstations, or other hubs. Many switches have ports for different speeds such as 10 Mbps Ethernet and 100 Mbps Fast Ethernet in the same unit.
- Category 1 (Cat 1) Cable: Unshielded Twisted Pair (UTP) for analog telephone; not suitable for data.
- Category 3 (Cat 3) Cable: UTP for data rates up to 10 Mbps (minimum for 10—BaseT Ethernet).
- Category 5 (Cat 5) Cable: UTP for data rates up to 100 Mbps (Fast Ethernet) recommended for networks.
- Thinnet (thin Ethernet): Coax cable 5mm thick for nodes up to 1,000 feet apart (10Base2).
- Thicknet (thick Ethernet): Coax cable 1 cm in diameter for nodes up to 3,300 feet apart.
- 10BaseT: IEEE standard for running Ethernet over twisted pair wires.

NETWORK OPERATING SYSTEMS (NOS)

The network operating system is the software that allows computers to communicate over local area networks. There are two major architectures for the NOS: client/server and peer-to-peer.

In standard client/server architecture, a piece of software resides on both the server and the client (the local PC). The server system software coordinates many functions such as network administration, security, file sharing, data protection, power monitoring, error detection, and control. The client portion of the NOS is loaded on each local PC, allowing that device to be connected to the network and providing a user interface with the server software. Examples of client/server network operating systems include Windows NT, Novell Netware, and Banyan Vines.

In peer-to-peer networks a part of the NOS software is loaded on each PC or workstation which runs on top of the PC operating system. Peer-to-peer networks do not require a central server or servers, and each PC may act as a file server while doing other things. Examples of peer-to-peer network operating systems include LANtastic, Windows for Workgroups, and Personal Netware.

BROADBAND NETWORKS (WIDE AREA NETWORKS)

Broadband networks, also known as wide area networks (WANs), are communications networks spanning large areas by using telecommunications lines running different protocols (e.g., frame relay, ATM, X.25, TCP/IP). Metropolitan area networks (MANs) are a type of broadband network that usually operates within an urban area. Libraries may want to consider that some of the key services in broadband networks include:

- ISDN (Integrated Services Digital Network): A worldwide standard for digital communications networks and can transmit voice, video, audio, and data. ISDN was originally developed in 1984 and is widely deployed in Europe and sections of the United States. The lowest data rates in this standard are 2/64Kbps circuits.

- BISDN (Broadband Integrated Services Digital Network): High-speed communication standard. BISDN services include frame relay, SMDS (Switched Multimegabit Data Services) and ATM (Asynchronous Transfer Mode).

- X.25: A CCITT standard that defines a protocol for gaining access to public packet switching networks. Developed in 1976, this is now an older protocol which is being replaced by frame relay, ATM, etc. This technology was used by OCLC in its national network redesign in the early 1990s, but it is now being replaced by TCP/IP services.

- Frame relay: A CCITT standard for packet switching running at speeds from 56Kbps to 2 Mbps. It has better efficiency and higher throughput than X.25. It supports bandwidth-on-demand (burst rates) which can go above the committed information rate (CIR) which has been licensed. Most metropolitan areas have frame relay "clouds," and one connects to a nearby node.

- SMDS (Switched Multmegabit Data Service): A high-speed metropolitan area network (MAN) service offered by many phone companies in larger urban areas. It supports speeds of up to 34 Mbps. As a backbone service this will be replaced by ATM.

- ATM (Asynchronous Transfer Mode): A cell-relay method used by BISDN for high-speed data transmission to over 2 Gbps. It offers packet switching at different speeds and is not associated with a single media (e.g. fiber, copper). ATM, which uses fixed length data packets, is being increasingly employed by academia, industry, and other high-end users.

SONET: SYNCHRONOUS OPTICAL NETWORKS

SONET network technology was originally developed by Bellcore and is an advanced optical fiber-based network defined by a large family of technical standards. Large companies, universities, and cities are the primary users. It features very high transmission speeds, excellent functionality, and, once installed, low maintenance of the physical plant. SONET networks may carry many different protocols such as frame relay, ATM, SMDS, FDDI, and ISDN packets. Most of the Internet2 development for a high-speed network for higher education is based on implementing SONET technology for segments of the Internet.

SONET multiplexers are compatible with existing telecommunications infrastructure with both synchronous and asynchronous electrical interfaces. SONET topologies include ring networks, star networks, point-to-point networks, and hybrid networks.

TCP/IP AND THE INTERNET PROTOCOLS

The Transmission Control Protocol/Internet Protocol (TCP/IP) was originally developed by the Defense Advance Research Projects Agency (DARPA) in the 1970s to link the United States government with its contractors over the early Internet. TCP/IP is a set of protocols and standards, and defines such services as listed here:

- File transfer (ftp)
- Terminal emulations and connections (telnet)
- Electronic mail (SMTP)
- Network management (SNMP)
- Hypertext transfer protocol (http), in use since 1993, is used for the World Wide Web

TCP/IP is the protocol used on the Internet and is the standard of choice for most internetworking between LANs and WANs. Most organizations are now running TCP/IP networks or are running internal proprietary protocols (such as IPX for Novell) with gateways to the broader IP network. TCP/IP packets may be embedded within other high-speed network protocols such as frame relay and ATM.

One of the dilemmas facing libraries in the virtual library environment is choosing when electronic services should be accessed over the open Internet as opposed to leasing a dedicated line. Certain criteria may help in this decision process:

- How critical is the database or service? For example, if a large university has many people involved with cataloging and ILL through OCLC, and if the service is unreliable or unstable over the university's open Internet account, then a dedicated line may make sense.
- Is there enough bandwidth for your institution over the open Internet? How bad and frequent are slowdowns during peak periods?
- Is your Internet service nearby (from a network perspective) to key electronic services that must be accessed?
- Is your Internet Service Provider (ISP) stable and reliable?
- How good is support through your institution for the Internet?
- Do you have a choice? Even if there are failures or weaknesses in the above tests, some organizations do not give particular departments or divisions (e.g., the library) a choice in ISP selection.

Another major challenge facing libraries is how to offer remote access for users who may be needing access from their home, office, or outside the library walls. Clearly many have dial-up access through commercial Internet Service Providers (e.g., America Online, CompuServe, EarthLink, Prodigy, and others), but libraries sometimes also need to provide their own. Academic libraries will usually work with the campus computer center for support of this kind of service. Public libraries, typically, do not have the ability to go to their city for this kind of service so it must be supported either by themselves, through a consortial affiliation offering this service, or through special arrangements with a commercial ISP. Most libraries are moving away from character-based dial-ins and preferring dial-up support for TCP/IP access for graphical browser support. Serial Line Internet Protocol (SLIP) is an older standard for this kind of dial-in support for IP access. Most newer dial-in services use PPP (point-to-point protocol) for IP support. Since many commercial electronic resources use IP filtering for authentication, an institutional modem pool works especially well for this type of security. If a library does not have access to an institutional modem pool, then IP filtering authentication will not work for home users and more sophisticated authentication techniques will be necessary.

Some libraries are still using older "dumb" terminals or PCs for character-based access to their integrated library system. Older telecommunication protocols such as X.25 are still in use in some areas. As libraries work on converting to TCP/IP, it is sometimes necessary to use devices such as protocol translators as an interim step. Protocol translation is a technique to convert one packet protocol (e.g., X.25) to another (e.g., TCP/IP). It is often done via software in a router and is needed until a library can afford to upgrade to a newer protocol. Protocol translation is also done between LANs running a proprietary protocol and the broader Internet via a gateway.

Many libraries must use the Internet Service Provider that has been selected by their parent organization and have little or no influence in ISP selection. However, where a library can make a selection or have influence on ISP selection there are several factors that should be taken into consideration:

- Examine the major electronic resources to which you will be connecting. What ISPs do they use and how far away are they from a networking perspective (e.g., how many hops in a trace route)?
- Does the ISP provide network management, statistics, line monitoring, and other technical support if there are problems?
- Does the ISP offer adequate bandwidth, and does it have potential to grow?
- Is the ISP a reseller for another service? If so, to whom do they connect and what value-added services do they offer?
- What is the reliability and stability of the service? Ask for a partial customer list to talk with other users of their service.

Another popular trend among libraries is to develop private or internal Internet services called an Intranet. Intranets are usually based around a Web server and are typically used for internal documentation, internal databases, staff support, and training. Since many libraries now have PCs available to every staff person, using an Intranet for staff support is an excellent technique for communication and documenting policies. There are no papers to lose, and the latest edition of documents can always be available online. One of the challenges of Intranets is the issue of security.

If important documents are managed and distributed via this technique, it is important to properly secure documents and databases so that only appropriate people have access to what they need. The organization must also pay special attention to external security threats (e.g., hacking), and organizations often employ techniques such as "firewalls" which is a barrier established by a router or other software through which a broadcast cannot pass without proper authorization.

As the Internet has grown exponentially, a new version of TCP/IP called IP Version 6 has been introduced which will increase the number of IP addresses available for computers around the world. A problem facing users is that the number of top level domain names is limited because of a limited number of suffixes in historical use. For example .edu is used by educational institutions; for-profit companies use .com; .org is used by nonprofit companies; and .net is used by Internet service providers. Whole new bodies of generic top level domains (gTLD) have been approved for use:

.firm	for businesses or firms
.shop	for businesses offering goods to purchase
.web	for entities emphasizing cultural and entertainment activities related to the Web
.art	for entities emphasizing art
.rec	for entities emphasizing recreation/entertainment
.info	for entities providing information services
.nom	for those wishing individual or personal nomenclature

The World Wide Web has become the interface of choice for most electronic resources. Although some companies still offer character-based interfaces (telnet) or Windows clients (e.g., WinSPIRS from SilverPlatter, SciFinder from the American Chemical Society), the Web browser is the predominant user interface. Netscape Navigator and Microsoft's Internet Explorer have emerged as the leading browsers although some use is made of older browsers and alternative browsers (e.g., Opera). Some academic institutions still promote a character-based browser called LYNX with which a user can connect via a telnet session because of older equipment, older dial-in lines (which do not support SLIP or PPP), or for visually impaired users since it is easier to voice synthesize a character-based LYNX interface.

INTERNET2

Internet2 is a collaborative effort in higher education in the United States to "Facilitate and coordinate the development, deployment, operation and technology transfer of advanced networked-based applications and network services to further U.S. leadership in research and higher-education and accelerate the availability of new services and applications on the Internet" (http://www.internet2.edu). This collaborative effort between higher education and industry to create a new high-speed gigabit TCP/IP network has been in the discussion stage for several years. This development effort was finally formalized in October 1997 through the creation of the University Corporation for Advanced Internet Development (UCAID). Doug Van Houweling, formerly with the University of Michigan, was selected as the first CEO. The original plans for Internet2 were announced in October 1996 and included thirty-four research universities. Under UCAID the membership base has broadened to 116 regular members in November 1997 with over 35 corporate members and more than twenty affiliated organizations. Although the general goals of Internet2 have remained unchanged since its inception, they are being formalized under UCAID (http://www.ucaid.edu):

- Demonstrate new applications that can dramatically enhance researchers' ability to collaborate and conduct experiments.
- Demonstrate enhanced delivery of education and other services (e.g., health care environmental monitoring) by taking advantage of "virtual proximity" created by an advanced communications infrastructure.
- Support development and adoption of advanced applications by providing middleware and development tools.
- Facilitate development, deployment, and operation of an affordable communications infrastructure, capable of supporting differentiated Quality of Service (QoS) based on applications requirements of the research and education community.
- Promote experimentation with the next generation of communications technologies.
- Coordinate adoption of agreed working standards and common practices among participating institutions to ensure end-to-end quality of service and interoperability.

- Catalyze partnerships with governmental and private sector organizations.
- Encourage transfer of technology from Internet2 to the rest of the Internet.
- Study impact of new infrastructure, services and applications on higher education and the Internet community in general.

Internet2 is not meant to replace the existing Internet but to provide high-speed service to participating institutions in higher education. It is being developed in local and regional pieces, as institutions are able to fund the high-speed equipment and telecommunication lines. Selected bandwidth-intensive applications are being deployed in the early phases of Internet2 while other regular Internet traffic is still being largely done over standard Internet links.

ASYMMETRIC DIGITAL SUBSCRIBER LINES (ADSL) AND CABLE MODEMS

Asymmetric Digital Subscriber Line (ADSL) is a new technology which is part of a larger family of xDSL services which converts existing twisted-pair telephone lines into digital circuits capable of transmitting data at speeds up to 7 Mbps. Within the next decade ADSL technology will likely be used to provide high-speed data access at home or small businesses for voice, data, or many multimedia applications.

An ADSL circuit connects to an ADSL modem on each end of a twisted-pair telephone line creating three channels: a high-speed downstream channel, a medium-speed duplex channel, and a POTS (Plain Old Telephone Service) channel. The POTS channel is segmented from the digital modem by filters, thus guaranteeing regular telephone service even if the digital portion of ADSL fails. Downstream data rates depend on many factors, including the length of the copper line, its wire gauge, presence of bridged taps, and cross-coupled interference. Line attenuation increases with line length and frequency, and decreases with wire diameter increases.

ADSL uses advanced digital signal processing and compression algorithms to squeeze large amounts of data through regular telephone lines. It also uses many advances in analog filters, transformers, and A/D converters to operate. Frequency Division Multiplexing (FDM) is used to assign one band for upstream data and another band for downstream data. The downstream path is then split by time division multiplexing in high and low speed channels. ADSL will support many different packet protocols including the Internet Protocol and ATM transport (Asynchronous Transfer Mode).

Libraries have come to play key roles in most public and academic communities: as on-ramps to the Internet for the local community or academic environment and as providers of databases to their user community either through locally mounted services (e.g., online public access catalogs, locally loaded indexing/abstracting services, locally loaded full-text, local digitization projects), or as conduits for commercially licensed databases on the Internet.

The television cable industry is also gearing up to offer high-speed Internet service to home users through digital cable lines. Digital cable will allow cable TV users to attach a special cable modem to their incoming digital cable line which can then connect with a PC in the home. One of the digital cable channels will then be used as a two-way, high-speed communications line for Internet access.

High-speed Internet access at home—whether through xDSL services, cable modems, fiber optics from the telephone company, or just high-speed modems—will affect the virtual library in several ways. Librarians should consider several steps to serve users with high-speed Internet connections better:

- Obtain extra bandwidth for your institutional Internet service. Users will place increasing demands on network bandwidth with their higher speed connections.
- Offer new multimedia or other higher bandwidth Internet services. Historically, libraries have leaned towards the low-end user. However, as patrons use other cutting-edge Web sites, libraries may begin to pale in comparison unless they keep up.
- Acquire multiple ISPs to provide redundancy in your Internet services and to split traffic so that users have a relatively short path, from a network perspective, to your institutional Web site. For example, if an ADSL service becomes highly popular in your

customer base, you may want to connect your library or institution directly to the ADSL service to offer high performance.

NETWORK COMPUTERS USING THIN CLIENT ARCHITECTURE

Network Computers (NCs) using "thin client" architecture allow organizations to provide software applications over networked "smart terminals" connected to a central server. The server offers all applications to the workstations over the network and provides dynamic allocations of RAM and disk resources to each unit, depending on the applications being run by the user at each moment. Because these workstations are configured to work from the server, the unit cost for each device is theoretically lowered, and central management of software is possible. One of the other major advantages of this technology is that older 286, 386, or 486 PCs may be added to this type of network without upgrades to make them Windows compatible. This means that older PCs do not have to be "junked" or upgraded as quickly. Users on these "recycled" devices have the same high-end resources available to them as network users with newer equipment.

The thin client architecture has many different meanings in the industry. Major hardware and software mainstays such as IBM, Wyse, Oracle, Microsoft, and Sun, as well as firms such Citrix and Netscape, are developing strategies. Each has slightly different interpretations of what defines thin client architecture. To some, a thin client design may be viewed as application development and deployment in a Java or ActiveX environment so that the user only needs to use a Web browser to accomplish tasks without having to launch "thick" or "fat" Windows-based clients, which are custom-built. Others view thin clients more comprehensively as networked "terminals" (or stripped down PCs or even older PCs) which run a specialized thin client piece of software (or firmware on a terminal), often called middleware, with all software resources available from a central server. It is felt that in many larger corporate settings most users need a limited number of applications (e.g., word processing, spreadsheet, presentation software, Web browser, telnet client) and do not need a powerful dedicated CPU (exceptions would include, for example, engineering applications, multimedia authoring, and high resolution graphics work). It is sometimes less expensive to provide RAM, disk space, and even CD-ROMs over the network. The cost is not just the initial outlay but should be viewed over the entire life cycle of the PC— including support, new software distribution, training, repair, and upgrades.

In 1997 and early 1998, networked computers were considered very "hot" in the computing marketplace. However, with the advent of powerful, low cost (under $1,000) PCs, much of the networked computer emphasis disappeared. Large corporations (including libraries) which desire centralized control and support of PCs may find networked computer solutions attractive for centralized software updating and desktop support. However, many also feel that the low cost of PCs now more than offsets per-seat software costs which network computers require.

AUTHENTICATION

User authentication and authorization have long been issues that have been dealt with by the computing community. However, as libraries and other organizations have begun to develop a more comprehensive networked vision of information access over the Internet, it has become clear that flexible new solutions need to be implemented. Players in this drama must include the library patron, the library itself, the information provider, and sometimes other third parties. Further complicating the environment, many libraries are now involved in library consortia that are actively taking part in not only providing services but also brokering deals for member libraries in order to save money.

The goal in user authentication and authorization is to let valid parties access databases and information services from anywhere at anytime without making the process too difficult for the library, information provider, or patron.

Most libraries currently offer electronic information from a wide variety of sources, some of which require user authentication and authorization, and some information that can be for open access (e.g., the library catalog). For most libraries it is not unusual to have a mix of resources such as an open access library online catalog, networked CD-ROMs which require authentication, access to electronic journals from a variety of publishers or aggregators which require authentication, access to a variety of indexing and abstracting services from remote providers (e.g., OCLC FirstSearch, IAC,

EBSCO, UMI ProQuest, Dialog@CARL), access to a variety of databases which are locally mounted but require authentication (e.g., SilverPlatter, Ovid, OCLC SiteSearch), or access to a mix of other networked resources requiring authentication (e.g., *Encyclopedia Britannica*, *Encyclopedia Americana*, Chadwyck-Healey LION, Intelex, or a host of others). To further complicate matters, libraries want to provide access to workstations not only in the library (and on campus if in an academic institution) but to their users at home and in the office or dorm. Some organizations provide their own dial-in modem pools (which would likely have the same network identity as on-campus workstations) but many organizations do not. In addition, many organizations are beginning to outsource dial-in service to commercial organizations and many valid patrons have selected commercial Internet Service Providers (e.g., AOL, CompuServe, Prodigy, MSN, or EarthLink). IP filtering alone is not a fully adequate authentication technique.

Most libraries are using their World Wide Web home pages to organize and explain to the library customer what is available and how it can be accessed. It is also common to explain on the library Web pages what access restrictions apply, and it is often here that the library must explain the complexities of why some databases may or may not be accessed because of authorization and authentication challenges.

A variety of general solutions for authentication have been commonly employed—each with its own benefits and limitations.

IP Filtering

In the technique known as "IP filtering," an IP address (or range of addresses) is used to filter access to a database or service so that only authorized users may gain access. IP filtering may take place on server where the information resides, or on some other server between the user and the resource. The benefit of this solution is that it is very easy to implement (a whole institutional class B or set of class C IP domains can be handled at once); and from the user perspective there are no passwords to remember, no unauthorized giving out of passwords to others, and the library or IP does not need to manage a large set of dynamically changing passwords. The major problem with reliance on IP filtering alone is that many users may be using commercial ISPs which do not have the same network domain as their institution and thus cannot be used for access. This means that the patron must either come onto campus or into the library to gain access, or dial in through an institutional modem pool. Although IP filtering is one of the most widely used techniques, if used alone it fails the test of "access from anywhere." A library has partially failed if a user must physically drive into the organization and cannot use the resources from their home (through a commercial ISP) or office, or while out of town on a trip.

ID Login and Password

For many years, the computing community has depended on the use of logins and passwords to control access to computer systems. In this technique, the user is asked to login for access. To improve security, passwords must be periodically changed to cut down on unauthorized users who may have somehow acquired passwords. Although this technique works well, it has many challenges: the issuing of logins and passwords can be a huge job especially in a larger library setting (many times users are asked to use their library ID card number), and passwords can be distributed by patrons to unauthorized users. If random logins/passwords are issued, they are often forgotten and one may end up with many passwords for different systems (unless handled through a gateway or proxy server).

Proxy Servers

In the "proxy server" technique, a user must login or pass an IP filter into an intermediate server which is automatically known by the end IP as only passing a legitimate user. Basically, users on one machine are allowed to be passed to another. This technique has been widely used, especially for telnet or Z39.50 connections where users take on the identity of the last server they passed through. Although this technique is possible in the Web environment, it is much more difficult because in a traditional Web connection one typically retains the network identity of your browser.

Proxies have a number of limitations. They can become a single point of failure in an organization so that if the proxy is down, all access to everyone is gone. Proxy servers mean that all requests are handled twice, meaning extra overhead in computer processing and sometimes response time problems. In a Web environment one must specially configure a browser to use a proxy rather than going directly to the end provider. Proxy solutions work when one has a clearly defined "parent organization," and this can become problematic because patrons will often have multiple affiliations and many libraries have multiple affiliations (e.g., members of different consortia or societies).

Kerberos

"Kerberos is a cryptographic authentication scheme designed for secure use over public computer networks. Through the exchange of encrypted messages called tickets, a user on the network can be authenticated against a centrally administered database of accounts and passwords in such a way that a user's password is never sent unencrypted over the computer network" (Garrison, 1997, p. 52). Using Kerberos or similar software, a central database of users and passwords may be maintained for all database or information access. Some of the benefits of this type of solution are that one only needs one password for access to all resources so that a user does not need to keep track of several logins and passwords; if a change or update needs to be made to a person's account, it can be done once for everything so that all authentication is "in sync" everywhere; many times a social security number, library card number, or other institutional ID can be used so that a patron may already know their number; and the privacy of the patron is ensured through encryption. Some of the obvious issues with a Kerberos-style solution are that one must have staff to handle the support and maintenance of this type of centralized software; if a patron has an incorrect or bad record, he is locked out of everything; and in an academic setting the library is usually not in charge of this type of solution so that one must live with the rules, regulations, and limitations of the department in charge which may or may not have the same philosophy of service and access as the library.

Electronic Certificates

The Internet Engineering Task Force (IETF) and others are working on various types of electronic certificates for authentication purposes. Standard X509 (now in Version 3) uses a technique where "the person (workstation) in possession of this digital object has this name (where name is interpreted rather loosely, and might include a public crypto-graphic key that the individual can use to sign documents)...the traditional use of certificates is for authentication and not authorization. There are provisions to carry user attributes in X509 Version 3 certificates, for example, but there are no standards on what attributes should be carried or how to interpret them" (Lynch, 1997, p. 35). Typically, an electronic certificate would carry enough information so that a user could then be authorized (because of their affiliation with a university, for example) against a central database for access to a suite of resources. Both Netscape and Microsoft are beginning to incorporate electronic certificate software in their browsers as this type of need grows.

Patron authentication and authorization issues are becoming increasingly complex as libraries move into a distributed and networked information environment. No solution is universal and different approaches are needed by different organizations to meet local needs. It is important that a library or consortium clearly define its needs. The goal in user authentication and authorization is to let valid parties access databases and information services from anywhere at anytime without making the process too difficult for the library, information provider, or patron. Flexibility is needed on both the part of information providers to allow different solutions to meet institutional needs and by libraries who need to incorporate reasonable security.

CONCLUSION

The library and the evolving virtual library have important roles to play in the information society. Libraries serve as a major database and service provider not only to the electronic library catalog but also to database subscriptions, special collections, and local resources. Public libraries in particular act as an "on ramp" to the Internet for many of the "have nots" in our society. The library should also play a key role in organizing electronic resources of interest to a local community in order to minimize confusion in our complicated electronic world. Some of the key challenges for libraries include the controversy over filtering Web resources for children, how to handle remote authentication/authorization services for remote users, how to handle training and education for electronic resources, and how to move more fully into the digital library realm so that authorized users can get the information they need when they need it.

References

Garrison, W. V. & McClellan, G. A. (1997). Tao of gateway: Providing Internet access to licensed databases. *Library Hi Tech, 15* (1-2), 39-54.

Lynch, C. A. (1997). The changing role in a networked information environment. *Library Hi Tech, 15* (1-2), 30-38.

Recommended Resources

Davidson, R. P. (1994). *Broadband networking ABCs for managers: ATM, BISDN, Cell/Frame Relay to SONET*. New York: Wiley.

Machovec, G. S. (1993). *Telecommunications, networking and Internet glossary*. Chicago: Library and Information Technology Association.

Miller, M. A. (1995). *Internetworking: A guide to network communications LAN to LAN; LAN to WAN*, 2d ed. New York: M & T Books.

Shafer, K. (1997). *Novell's dictionary of networking*. San Jose, CA: Novell Press.

The Evolving Virtual Library:
A Vision, Through a Glass, Darkly

Marshall Keys, Ph.D.
Executive Director
NELINET
Newton, Massachusetts

We are building the virtual library of the future within the shell of the library of today. What is happening in the most advanced libraries now will become common practice across all types of libraries within fifteen years. This will occur in the same way that the adoption of OPACs and local systems, advanced telecommunications, and electronic resources (first introduced by advanced libraries beginning in the early 1980s) became the basic expectations of all libraries by the late 1990s.

Libraries today are very different from the libraries of 1980, although we are so familiar with the changes and have lived through them so gradually that we are not ordinarily aware of how different they have become. These changes will continue. However, the library of 2010 will be more different from the library of today than the library of today is different from the library of 1980, even though we may be equally unable to recognize the depth of change as it happens. But when we look back from 2010, we will be able to see that really revolutionary change has taken place. The seeds of these changes are being cast onto fertile ground in the 1990s. Whether the crop will turn out to be corn or kudzu is the real question, and one we will not, of course, be able to determine until time for the harvest.

The evolving virtual library will have many familiar features. It will still, in most cases, continue to be a physical place. It will still have collections, and it will still have staff. The way it acquires those collections, the way it provides access to them, the composition of the staff, and the nature of the work they do, are likely to be quite strikingly different. The process through which these changes come about will not always be smooth and will not always be pleasant. As we live through this, it will be important to remind ourselves that the library of 2010 will be the product of an enormously expansive process. The next decade will add greatly to the scope of what libraries take on, what they do, and what they are able to deliver to their users. We will be like librarians in the early days of printing, attempting to cope with a whole new medium, a whole new kind of commerce, and a whole new set of bibliographic issues (many of which are the same as they were in 1500—provenance, authority, authenticity, etc.). Our users will be as much better off in the library of 2010 as users of information after Gutenberg were better off than their medieval predecessors. Far more information will be available in the virtual library to far more people with far less effort than today. But the process of transition will not be easy for librarians.

Virtual Libraries, Digital Libraries, Electronic Collections

What do we mean by the term "virtual library?" In common use the term "virtual library" usually implies a library that provides access to a collection of distributed information in electronic format through pointers provided locally. We also hear the term "digital library" used interchangeably with "virtual library," though to some writers, "digital library" implies a collection of digital objects housed in the same place, virtual or physical. Don Waters (1998), director of the Digital Library Federation, defines the term "digital library" in organizational terms:

> Digital libraries are organizations that provide the resources, including specialized staff, to select, organize, provide intellectual access to, distribute, preserve the integrity of, and ensure the persistence over time of collections of digital works so that they are readily and economically available for use by a defined community or set of communities.

Waters' definition places more emphasis on the organization that offers digital collections and services than on the collections and services themselves. In this chapter, I will use all three terms almost interchangeably, relying on the good sense of the reader to discern my meaning at any given point and on the future to clarify the definition beyond ambiguity.

LIBRARIES TODAY AND TOMORROW

Tomorrow's library will not differ superficially too much from today's. The library of today is already what Chris Rusbridge (1998) calls a "hybrid library"—one that holds and provides access to materials in all kinds of formats. Nor will the virtual library be separate from the analog libraries in which we now work. Sidney Verba, University Librarian at Harvard, says, "The term 'digital library' gives the impression that there is a separate library that is unconnected to the old-fashioned library housing books and journals. This is quite the opposite of what we have in mind. [W]e think of our Library as having many different media" (Hanke, 1998).

Libraries of the future will continue to be libraries with mixed collections as long as we can imagine. We will continue to have legacy collections in paper, transition collections of materials digitized from paper, and collections of vast amounts of newly created paper, all existing alongside the digital resources we point to from our local systems. How then will these libraries differ from today's library?

The most fundamental difference is that the locus of control over the library's collection will begin to move outside the library itself as the proportion of distributed resources rises in the collection. When libraries lease or license a large proportion of their total resources, control of the collection becomes vested in other institutions and organizations. This change in the locus of control over library collections will have many manifestations, and because librarianship as a profession is all about the issue of control, it will cause much stress and distress among librarians.

First, because digital collections will be stored off site, the individual library will have far less control than today over the actual availability of information to the end user. The library will be completely dependent for what users retrieve at any given time on the provider of the data, the designer of the search engine, the provider of the bandwidth required to connect to the data, the local area network manager, and the designer of the interface.

The failure of any of these components means the failure of the virtual library to deliver information, and none of these components is under the control of the library itself. Contrast this to the situation ten years ago when almost all the resources of libraries were physical materials that were owned and stored on site or borrowed and loaned as physical objects, whether returnable or not.

Secondly, distributed digital collections are licensed, rather than owned by the library that points to them, and libraries will share the use of these collections with other institutions, not only locally but around the world. The locus of control over standards for digital collections—standards for inclusion, standards of presentation, and standards for such things as authentication, authority control, and preservation—is no longer in the library but somewhere outside it. In the best case, the standards will be developed, maintained, and asserted by professional organizations; in the worst case, they will be the sole creation of individuals or organizations whose primary interest is revenue. Even in the best case, however, standards will have to reflect world practice rather than local or even national practice, and librarians will have to accept data in formats that may be unfamiliar and unwelcome.

Moreover, digitally created objects (as contrasted to transitional digital documents that have an origin or parallel in paper) will soon be self-describing. They will not be cataloged but will carry self-generated metadata descriptions. They will not be cataloged in the traditional way because the number of digital objects being created will quickly outstrip the number of catalogers available to catalog them. In addition, the level of granularity at which digital objects may be retrieved is simply too fine for conventional cataloging to cope with. The search engine is more powerful with retrieval than traditional access created by the human cataloger.[1] The locus of control for intellectual access to the collection is also passing outside the library, at least at the level of the individual resource.

Third, what gets published, what a library adds to its "collections" when it points to a digital resource, will also be the result of remote and often collective, rather than individual, decision making. What is available digitally will be what finds ready acceptance in the market. Libraries now have and are paying for electronic journals from Academic Press simply because their journals are only available as part of a package; take one, and you take them all. Academic Press is a reputable organization, but we can see from other current experience that the factors that lead to wide distribution in the marketplace may have nothing to do with quality, authority, or persistence and everything to do with price, advertising, and ease of use.

Finally, access to retrospective materials has been at the core of the library's role as the guardian of the cultural record. In the future, access to these materials will be neither free nor certain as control of them passes out of the hands of the library. Barring invasion, fire, or flood, library resources have been considered "permanent," surviving at least as long as the culture that values them. Many thousands of incunabula survive from the Middle Ages in libraries, and libraries quite regularly shelve books that are two-hundred-years old on open shelves, accessible to the public. The archiving of digital collections will depend on the continued corporate existence of those who own the rights to them. And while there are companies that are three-hundred-years old, none of them (to my knowledge) is a commercial publisher.[2] How long will J-STOR and OCLC ECO survive? And what then?

Even if archiving organizations survive over extended periods of time, access to the materials they hold will continue to require access fees, either subscription or transaction based. These fees may well be less than the cost of storing information on site in either paper or electronic format, but we do not yet know, nor are we likely to know in the next ten years.

These changes in the locus of control over library collections are likely to be stressful, even to those librarians who stop to understand the issue and develop strategies to cope with it. Most librarians will not; they will only deal with its effects, which may be overwhelming. The most immediate effects will certainly include the accelerated transformation of much of the work done in libraries. We will see further differentiation between the production work of libraries (much of it becoming automated or outsourced) and the professional work, work which is characterized by abstract thinking, communication, planning, and evaluating. Librarians will continue to need foundation in the concepts of librarianship, but they will also need managerial skills, the ability to analyze practice and synthesize new concepts to apply to it. They will need to be knowledgeable about library issues but they will also need to be skilled in much broader areas (planning, negotiating, persuading, and so forth) that are not part of the present library school curriculum.

As librarians take on these primarily intellectual tasks, still more of the work of production in the library will migrate to paraprofessionals, not without consequences for libraries as organizations. Professor Sheila Intner (1995) of Simmons College has spoken with considerable eloquence of those who do what they define as the "real work" of libraries, work formerly done by professional librarians, while the librarians themselves, who are better paid, seem to sit at their computers staring into space, talk on the telephone, and go to meetings all day. This kind of intellectual and collaborative activity—understanding the environment and creating responses to it—is becoming the real work of librarians as it is the real work of knowledge workers everywhere. Library work is responding to outside forces at an accelerating rate, and those who will be most affected in the next decade do not necessarily understand the skills they will need to cope.

THE NEW INFORMATION ECONOMY

The ultimate shape of the virtual library will depend on interactions among five complex factors:

1. The economics of publishing
2. The course of development of metadata
3. The status of information aggregators
4. The development of local system technology
5. The place of consortia in the environment

We cannot predict the outcome of development in any of these fields at this point, but we can outline the issues which librarians need to track if we are to be prepared for the future.

The Economics of Publishing

Librarians can spin endless scenarios about the future of electronic scholarly publishing.[3] In the most benign, colleges and universities declare all faculty research to be "work done for pay," allowing institutions to claim copyright for written material as they now do for patents. The institution then cooperates with libraries and scholarly associations to make this material available to the world at low cost. The opposite scenario, and the one that evokes the greatest sense of irony, has publishers breaking up journals and charging high fees for individual articles, most of which are never sold because, like doctoral dissertations, they are so specialized as to have very little financial value. Either or both scenarios could happen. What is unlikely to happen is any scenario based on publishers, particularly STM (Scientific-Technical-Medical) publishers, reducing prices voluntarily. This ignores the economics of the publishing industry at the turn of the century. To demonstrate this point, let us look at a case study in the economics of publishing.

As I write this, Reed Elsevier (1998) has announced that it is revamping its management, looking for a new CEO, and examining the core structure of its corporate relationship (now an Anglo-Dutch holding company in which power is equally divided). According to *The Wall Street Journal*, Reed Elsevier is taking these drastic steps because "its massive investments [in electronic publishing] have yet to pay off, and its profit margins are shrinking" (Frank, 1998, B7). According to the Journal, pretax profits for the first six months of 1998 were $675.9 million, a very large figure indeed but apparently not one that satisfies the joint owners. These revenues are down 1 percent from the previous year, and this is enough to require a complete corporate reorganization.

It is almost impossible for librarians to imagine that a profit of $675.9 million for half a year could be considered a negative result, but the real problem is the effect that this news has on Reed Elsevier stock prices. At the time I write, Reed's stock is down about 30 percent for the year, Elsevier's about 28 percent—enough to get the critical attention of shareholders, of investment analysts, and of the companies' managers themselves, who are compensated to a large extent with stock. Under these circumstances, it is certain that Reed Elsevier will not willingly do anything that is likely to reduce profitability in their high margin STM business, thus making continued high subscription prices to libraries a certainty until competition—business, political, or technological—challenges their dominance. Since all commercial publishers are ultimately answerable to shareholders or private owners, librarians cannot expect them to relinquish their dominance in the information marketplace without a fight.

The Development of Metadata

To date, publishers have focused primarily on obtaining and enforcing copyright as their chief method for retaining their dominant position in the information economy. Librarians are familiar with these issues and have vigorously opposed the efforts of the publishing community (most notably the Association of American Publishers) to limit fair use in the electronic environment. Librarians have had mixed success in fighting the effort of information industry lobbyists in the United States, and when the lobbyists carry the struggle to international venues, hoping to secure by treaty what they cannot do in the United States by statute, the battle becomes unequal.

More recently, beginning in the software industry, the focus has turned to licensing intellectual products for use rather than selling them outright to users. Librarians have become familiar with the restrictions placed by vendors around the use of electronic journals and reference sources, but computer software users have been required to sign licenses that restrict them even from disclosing the results of benchmark tests and from publishing reviews without the prior consent of the licenser. Proposed revisions of the Uniform Commercial Code are designed to extend the rights of vendors at the expense of consumers (Gleick, 1998).

A more insidious threat comes from the concept of metadata. Librarians are familiar with the idea of metadata—data about data—as an analog of cataloging applicable to electronic publications. As such, it has been of little interest to anyone other than specialists. But metadata is being defined and implemented in ways that pose challenges to libraries and their users through the development of digital object identifiers (DOIs).

As described by the International DOI Foundation (see http://www.doi.org), the Digital Object Identifier (DOI) System is an identification system for digital media...designed to provide persistent and reliable identification of digital objects via a proven technology—the CNRI Handle System—and an efficient administration system, to link customers with publishers, facilitate electronic commerce, and enable automated copyright management systems.

The Handle System on which DOIs are based "is a distributed computer system which stores names, or handles, of digital items and which can quickly resolve those names into the information necessary to locate and access the items" (see http://www.handle.net/index.html). It was developed by the Corporation for National Research Initiatives and applied to DOI's in a joint project with R.R. Bowker under the auspices of the Association of American Publishers.

DOIs allow the identification of any digital object at any level specified by the owner. Where an ISBN identifies a book at the title level and a URL identifies at the site and document level, a DOI can identify a digital object at the chapter, paragraph, sentence, phrase, abstract, footnote, table, chart, or illustration level. Unlike URLs, DOIs are persistent, and they can carry ownership and rights information as easily as they can carry identification or watermark information. Since the DOI remains a permanent part of the digital object it identifies, this metadata remains capable of identifying the ownership of information and of authorizing or refusing to authorize its use through multiple transfers (Powell, 1997).

The implications of DOIs for purchasers and users of information can be glimpsed in an article by Godfrey Rust (1998) in *D-Lib Magazine*. Rust notes that metadata is ordinarily thought of as a tool for discovering information and, as such, has been viewed as the province of the librarian. His article describes the advantages for rights holders of linking discovery and rights data in a single structure. In an electronic environment, "metadata is a critical agent, a glue which holds the pieces together." It "offers the opportunity to integrate the functions of discovery, access, licensing and accounting into single point-and-click actions" (Introduction). He then goes on to enumerate in great detail the elements that would be necessary to fully automate commerce in digital objects.

The advantages of this system to publishers are obvious. Through digital object identifiers, they can identify, track, and license digital information at any level of granularity. And what will the unit be? Music publishers have successfully sued record companies over the use of digital samples—musical phrases lifted digitally from one record and used as an element in creating another—and there is no reason to believe that other valuable digital objects would not be licensed at the same level of granularity if the DOI system gains wide acceptance. Thus a user who finds a likely article on the Web might be charged one fee for looking at an abstract, a second fee for reading the entire article, a third fee for downloading one or more portions of the article, and yet another fee for passing digital copies of these items on to a second user.

Elsevier has recently decided to allow libraries under fair use to create and send paper copies for interlibrary loan of materials from electronic journals to which the library subscribes. This gives libraries a certain amount of flexibility in supplying users, but library copying under fair use is a minuscule fraction of all transactions involving copying and distribution of copyrighted materials. If Elsevier were to apply DOIs to their electronic publications, it would almost certainly have the effect of drastically reducing the amount of wholesale electronic copying and transfer that would otherwise occur. Reed Elsevier owns R.R. Bowker, one of the developers of the DOI. Publishers will not willingly give up revenue streams without a fight, and DOIs give them the weapon for the battle.

Again, all this may go for naught if most digital objects lack value. How many of the articles—to say nothing of paragraphs—currently purchased by libraries have value or are even read? Most of what libraries buy is acquired only as part of a package that contains, or is perceived to contain, information that is valuable enough to purchase on a regular basis through periodical subscriptions. Years of usage studies at institutions call into question the actual use of many items bought by libraries, and the only effect of the DOI may be to show that the emperor is naked. Sorting these questions out will be one of the great themes of the next decade.

The Status of Information Aggregators

Libraries have always been dependent on secondary publishers and indexing and abstracting services like Wilson, Psychological Abstracts, and ISI to give users intellectual access to the material contained in their collections. With the development of electronic full text, libraries have become increasingly dependent on information aggregators for access to information. Information aggregators collect information from its owners, attach a search engine and interface to it, and retail the results to libraries. It is a rapidly growing business, encompassing such familiar companies as SilverPlatter and UMI, and newer players such as EBSCO and Ovid. Some companies focus on particular niches (IAC), and some, like OCLC, are both owners and distributors of information.

Information aggregators are in a very shaky position because most of them do not own the information they are redistributing. When sales of *Books in Print* (*BIP*) began to slip after many libraries purchased it through LEXIS-NEXIS, Bowker simply removed *BIP* from the LEXIS-NEXIS database, leaving the company and its customers high and dry on very short notice. Some aggregators have better contracts with their suppliers, but each of them is dependent on vendors for more or less of the information they supply. It is always tempting for information owners to maximize their own profits by bringing distribution closer to home if they can do so through technology or a timely purchase.

The recent purchase of Ovid by Kluwer for $200 million demonstrates two facets of this issue. On the one hand it marks an admission by a major STM publisher that users want and need indexing and abstracting services. Users do not ask the question "I wonder what Kluwer published this week," and they do not do direct searches of publisher's own Web sites as a primary way of locating information. If Kluwer (or Elsevier) wants users to know what they publish, they are dependent on indexing and abstracting services. Kluwer has changed the nature of the game by buying its *own* indexing and abstracting service. The competition will certainly be watching closely to see if their decision was a good one, at which time other abstracting and indexing services will look like desirable purchases. On the other hand, the question is whether Ovid will continue to be a popular information aggregator with users now that it has become effectively a distribution arm for a publisher. Will Kluwer's journals show up more often in result sets than those of their competitors? If so, confidence in Ovid will decrease; if not, what is the advantage to Kluwer?

The information aggregation business is thus unstable and undergoing a period of rapid change. There is no reason to believe that it will be any more stable for the next few years. Librarians are likely to see familiar resources change from vendor to vendor, familiar vendors falling by the roadside, and new names emerging frequently. Librarians who are now focused on price and presentation when making database and full-text decisions will need also to look for stable, adequately funded partners with long-term commitments from their suppliers before making purchase decisions.

The Development of Integrated Local Systems

The development of integrated local systems based on Z39.50 and other emerging data search and presentation standards is essential if libraries are to manage the multiple electronic data streams that will be entering their libraries. Online systems will become even more important during the next decade and a half than they have been in the past, at least partly because they also have the potential for mitigating some of the effects of disruption in the aggregation business. Because the emerging integrated systems can cross search multiple systems and sites for information and present the resulting data in a common format, a library will be able to change the source of data simply by inputting a new URL (and signing a new contract!). Disruption of the chain to any particular vendor becomes less important because the data can come from anywhere, and users are not required to learn new search techniques (though the underlying search algorithms and processes may change radically).

Thus, integrated local systems can restore some of the balance of power with respect to information aggregators and owners to libraries. When the same data is available and searchable from multiple sources, it becomes a commodity distinguishable only by price. However, this makes the library as dependent on its local system vendor as it is currently on information aggregators, and the situation is no more stable.

All knowledgeable observers expect that a number of local system vendors will fail within the next decade. Which specific vendors will fail is the subject of gossip, speculation, and innuendo. The critical factors to survival are, of course, a sufficient number of profitable contracts and a sufficiently low cost of development and production to satisfy the financial expectations of owners. Because the only publicly traded local system vendor is Data Research Associates (DRA), it is the only vendor for which significant financial data is available.

DRA is apparently a sound, well-run company, though its results from quarter to quarter are largely dependent on factors beyond its control—the timely signing or renewal of a major contract, for example. Its stock has split once, it pays regular dividends, and it has had occasional run-ups in the share price that must have been rewarding for those who sold stock. However, its stock has recently drifted from the high teens to the $11.00-$12.00 range. If the stock were widely held, management would be under the same pressure from shareholders as we saw at Elsevier and Reed. Since it is not widely held, management can probably ride out the present price level.

All firms in the industry are affected by the same business factors, but we do not have the information to be certain how deep the pockets or patience of the owners are in bad times. When CLSI was sold a number of years ago to a company outside the library industry, it was resold within a relatively few years, reportedly because of disappointing financials. Given the price pressure in the library world, disruption in the local system business—firms exiting the business or going bankrupt—is quite likely. Because local systems are becoming even more crucial to the operation of libraries, librarians need a contingency plan in case their own vendor is one of those disrupted. As a number of the nation's premier research libraries learned when Ameritech abandoned NOTIS, no institution is free of this risk.

The Place of Consortia

Participating in consortia has been libraries' chief response to a confused and confusing information environment. Through their participation, libraries have been able to negotiate more favorable licensing agreements with publishers and to obtain more competitive prices than they could achieve by acting individually. Consortial negotiation has helped to establish rational policies and models for pricing, terms of use, multiple-site licensing, liability for misuse, and a host of other issues. By helping to establish a stable marketplace, this has helped both buyers and sellers of information. Through consortial purchasing, libraries have been able to gain access to resources far beyond their ordinary capacity or at a much lower price than they would ordinarily have spent. In the Colorado FirstSearch purchase, for example, small libraries were able to obtain unlimited use for $200 per year while the University of Colorado obtained unlimited use for $40,000 per year less than their previous expenditure (Bolt, 1998). Everyone benefited.

There are however, three problems with consortia that will need to be worked out over the next few years. The first is unrealistic expectations on the part of consortium members, combined with short term thinking on the part of vendors. Many librarians assume that the price of resources purchased through consortia should decline year after year; many vendors have made major price concessions in first contracts as a way of buying market share and driving out the competition. When these two meet at renewal, they have no common ground. This is the "Year 2 Problem," when the cost of renewing a service to which users have become accustomed may be two or three times as high as the initial cost, and it is extremely distressing to the purchaser. The second problem is the "disappearing resource" alluded to in my discussion of aggregators; the subscriber takes on a subscription with the expectation of getting certain products which the vendor is unable to deliver, often through no fault of its own. Finally, there is the issue for both the library and the information owner of dealing with multiple consortia.

Libraries are notorious in the information industry for consortium shopping. Because they all belong to many consortia, they often wait to see which consortium can deliver the best price. Because prices depend on the number and composition of the members of a consortium, these shifts are nightmares for vendors attempting to set firm prices. Ultimately, these tactics increase rather than decrease the cost of information. The solution may be fewer and larger consortia (e.g., ICOLC, SOLINET, etc.) or consortia that specialize in getting the best prices in certain specific areas (NELINET and *Encyclopedia Britannica,* NERL and Academic Press). Whatever the outcome, the growth or decline of consortia will be an important issue during the early years of the next century.

INTO THE FUTURE

Although this chapter has focused on the difficult issues that stand between today's library and tomorrow's virtual library, we should not forget that the result of coping with these difficulties will be vastly improved access to information resources by vastly expanded user communities. We can expect the virtual library to be the organization that identifies, selects, negotiates for, and provides access to an incredible range of information resources on our behalf. We can imagine large libraries as information channels that, like cable television channels, direct to us streams of data, multimedia, information, and even digital television programming in specialized subject areas. We can imagine small libraries serving as repositories for or even broadcasting local historical, scientific, and cultural content, all this to users wherever we happen to be, whenever we want access, by whatever means (public terminal, desktop computer, pocket computer, telephone terminal) we find it most convenient to receive. We have a lot to get through in the meantime, but we have not got more than we had in the last fifteen years. Those of us who have begun the process with our work over the last decades will see it completed by others, but completed it will be.

Notes

1. I for one am not too sanguine about the ability of automated agents to describe digital objects with the kind of nonmeaningful titles that are common in the humanities, but perhaps time will prove me wrong.

2. And can they afford to take on the task of archiving even if so inclined? What is the effect of *Thor Power Tool v Internal Revenue Service* when the inventory is held electronically?

3. Electronic scholarly publishing is the only kind of electronic publishing that matters in 1999 because it is the only kind for which the costs to the library are significant. This is likely to change by 2010.

References

Bolt, N. (1998, October 7). Presentation in Greensboro, NC.

Frank, R. (1998, August 7). Reed Elsevier to revamp management amid painful shift to electronic media. *Wall Street Journal* B7, col.1.

Gleick, J. (1998, May 10). It's your problem (not theirs). *New York Times Magazine.*

Hanke, T. (1998, June 4) Speaking volumes: professor Sidney Verba champions the university library. *Harvard University Gazette* (http://www.news.harvard.edu/hno.subpages/gazarch/hno.gazette. june.4.html).

Intner, S. (1995, November 8). Presentation at the Tufts University Library.

Powell, A. (1997, November). The digital object identifier system. *Library Technology, 2* (www.sbu.ac. uk/litc/lt/1997/news196.html)

Reed-Elsevier (1998, August 6). Unitary management structure for Reed Elsevier (http://www. reed-elsevier.com/introduction.htm).

Rusbridge, C. (1998, July/August). Towards the hybrid library. *D-Lib Magazine* (http://mirrored.ukoln. ac.uk/lis-jou...b/july98/rusbridge.html).

Rust, G. (1998, July/August). Metadata: The right approach. An integrated model for descriptive and rights metadata in e-commerce. *D-Lib Magazine* (http://www.dlib.org/dlib/july98/ rust/07rust.html).

Contributors

Maria S. Bonn has the job title of Interface Specialist with the Digital Library Production Service at the University of Michigan in Ann Arbor. She has worked with the project for two years. She has an MILS from the University of Michigan and a Ph.D. in English from the State University of New York at Buffalo. Her e-mail address is mbonn@umich.edu.

Tore Brattli is an academic librarian at the University Library of Tromsø in Norway. He has a M.Sc. in Mathematics and Computer Science from the University of Tromsø. You can visit his Web site at http://www.ub.uit. no/ansat te/tore/ and contact him by e-mail at Tore.Brattli@ub.uit.no.

Judith J. Field is a senior lecturer in the Library and Information Science Program at Wayne State University, Detroit, Michigan. Judith is a former president of the Special Libraries Association and is a frequent presenter at professional conferences. Her e-mail address is jfield@lisp.purdy.wayne. edu.

Marshall Keys is the executive director of NELINET in Newton, Massachusetts, and is a popular speaker at conferences. His column in *NELINET Newsletter* has become must reading for area librarians. His e-mail address is mkeys@nelinet.net.

George Machovec is the technical director for the Colorado Alliance of Research Libraries in Denver, Colorado. In 1998 George spoke about network infrastructure in a nationally broadcast teleconference for librarians. Prior to working for the Colorado Alliance, he was the Systems Librarian at Arizona State University. He can be contacted by e-mail at gmachove@coalliance.org.

Gail McMillan is the director of the Scholarly Communications Project and Head of Special Collections at the University Libraries, Virginia Polytechnic Institute & State University in Blacksburg. She has also served as the Team Leader for Serials and for Online Maintenance at Virginia Tech. She has an M.L.S. and an M.A. from the University of Maryland, in College Park. She can be reached by e-mail at gailmac@vt.edu.

Donald Napoli has served as the director of the St. Joseph County Public Library in South Bend, Indiana, since 1977. He received his MLS from The Catholic University of America. His home page is available at http://sjcpl. lib.in.us/homepage/AboutDJN.html, and his e-mail address is donald.napoli@ gomail.sjcpl.lib.in.us.

Laverna M. Saunders is the dean of the Library, Instructional and Learning Support at Salem State College in Salem, Massachusetts. She has edited two previous books on the virtual library and edits the "Internet Librarian" section of *Computers in Libraries* magazine. She has an M.L.S. from Rutgers University, an M.A. from Drew University, and an Ed.D. from the University of Nevada, Las Vegas. She can be reached at saunders@noblenet.org.

Vicky York is an associate professor and distance education coordinator at Montana State University Libraries in Bozeman, Montana. She was a National Faculty Exchange participant with the Western Commission for Higher Education and wrote *A Guide for Planning Library Integration into Distance Education Programs* for the Western Cooperative for Educational Telecommunications. Her e-mail address is vyork@montana.edu.

Joyce Kasman Valenza is the librarian at Springfield Township High School in Erdenheim, Pennsylvania. She has had more than twenty years of experience in K-12, both as a teacher and librarian. Joyce writes the weekly "tech.k12" column for *The Philadelphia Inquirer* and is the author of *Power Tools* (ALA Editions) and *Internet Searching Skills* (Schlessinger Media). Her home page is available at http://mciunix.mciu.k12.pa.us/~spjvweb and her e-mail address is joyce.valenza@phillynews.com.

Index

Other Books of Interest from Information Today, Inc.

Teaching with Technology:
Rethinking Tradition
Edited by Les Lloyd

This latest informative volume from the mind of Les Lloyd includes trailblazing contributions from the 1998 "Teaching with Technology" conference. The presentations—by some of the leading experts in the field—are divided into four categories: Cross-Discipline Use of Technology, the Web as a Tool in Specific Disciplines, Technology Management for Faculty and Administration, and Techniques for Enhancing Teaching in Cross-Discipline Courses. If your college or university needs to be on the cutting edge of the technology revolution, this book is highly recommended.

Hardbound • ISBN 1-57387-068-4 • $39.50

The Internet Library:
Case Studies of Library Internet Management and Use
Edited by Julie Still

This book covers the use of the Internet in both patron services and technical services. A wide range of case studies is brought together here to explore the potential uses of the Net in a variety of libraries and for a range of functions.

Softbound • ISBN 0-88736-965-0 • $37.50

Electronic Styles:
A Handbook for Citing Electronic Information
By Xia Li and Nancy Crane

The second edition of the best-selling guide to referencing electronic information and citing the complete range of electronic formats includes text-based information, electronic journals and discussion lists, Web sites, CD-ROM and multimedia products, and commercial online documents.

Softbound • ISBN 1-57387-027-7 • $19.99

The Essential Guide to Bulletin Board Systems
by Patrick R. Dewey

This book details the setup and operation of bulletin board systems, which are interactive computer databases. There are chapters on hardware and software selection, software applications for personal computers, operational problems, and working with the World Wide Web, as well as examples of bulletin board system operations. These chapters are followed by invaluable resources, such as a vendor list, Internet service providers, distributors, consultants, bulletin boards to call, and bulletin board system resources on the Internet.

Hardbound • ISBN 1-57387-035-8 • $39.50

Entertainment Technology and Tomorrow's Information Services
By Thomas E. Kinney
Clearly, the emerging U.S. National Information Infrastructure (NII) is being created as much to support interactive television, video-on-demand, multimedia CDs, video games, virtual reality theme parks, and other digital entertainment services as it is to deliver what most of us recognize as "information." Directed mainly at professionals involved with the development and delivery of information services, this book explores how that entertainment orientation—as reflected in specific emerging technologies—is likely to shape the information services of tomorrow.

Hardbound • ISBN 1-57387-006-4 • $34.90

Great Scouts!
CyberGuides for Subject Searching on the Web
By Nora Paul and Margot Williams
Great Scouts! is a cure for information overload. Authors Nora Paul (The Poynter Institute) and Margot Williams (*The Washington Post*) direct readers to the very best subject-specific, Web-based information resources. Thirty chapters cover specialized "CyberGuides" selected as the premier Internet sources of information on business, education, arts and entertainment, science and technology, health and medicine, politics and government, law, sports, and much more. With its expert advice and evaluations of information and link content, value, currency, stability, and usability, Great Scouts! takes you "beyond search engines"—and directly to the top sources of information for your topic. As a reader bonus, the authors are maintaining a Web page featuring updated links to all the sites covered in the book.

Softbound • ISBN 0-910965-27-7 • $24.95

K-12 Networking:
Breaking Down the Walls of the Learning Environment
Edited by Doris M. Epler
Networking has become a useful tool as well as a way of organizing people, their work, and their resource needs—and this is especially true of schools and school library media centers. The chapters of this book address hundreds of real concerns educators have about implementing various types of networks in the schools.

Hardbound • ISBN 0-938734-94-6 • $39.50

Administrative Computing in Higher Education
Edited by Les Lloyd
With the expansion of campus-wide information systems and networks comes the advent of administrative computing: the use of networked systems by administrative personnel. Educators and campus administrators directly involved in the planning, building, and management of administrative computing systems in colleges and universities discuss models of data sharing across systems, upgrading administrative software, selection and expansion of computing systems, and much more.

Softbound • ISBN 1-57387-007-2 • $39.50

Net Curriculum:
An Educator's Guide to Using the Internet
By Linda C. Joseph
Linda Joseph, popular columnist for *MultiMedia Schools* magazine, puts her K-12 and Internet know-how to work in this must-have book for teachers and school media specialists. This is a practical guide that provides dozens of exciting project ideas, plus information on accessing information, electronic publishing, researching online, copyright and fair use, student safety, and much more.

Softbound • ISBN 0-910965-30-7 • $29.95

Information Management for the Intelligent Organization, 2nd Edition
By Chun Wei Choo
The intelligent organization is one that is skilled at marshaling its information resources and capabilities, transforming information into knowledge, and using this knowledge to sustain and enhance its performance in a restless environment. The objective of this newly updated and expanded book is to develop an understanding of how an organization may manage its information processes more effectively in order to achieve these goals. This book is a must read for senior managers and administrators, information managers, information specialists and practitioners, information technologists, and anyone whose work in an organization involves acquiring, creating, organizing, or using knowledge.

Hardbound • ISBN 1-57387-057-9 • $39.50

Internet Blue Pages, 1999 Edition:
The Guide to Federal Government Web Sites
Compiled by Laurie Andriot
With over 900 Web addresses, this guide is designed to help you find any agency easily. Arranged in accordance with the US Government Manual, each entry includes the name of the agency, the Web address (URL), a brief description of the agency, and links to the agency's or subagency's home page. For helpful cross referencing, an alphabetical agency listing and a comprehensive index for subject searching are also included. Regularly updated information and links are provided on the author's Web site.

Softbound • ISBN 0-910965-29-3 • $34.95

The Extreme Searcher's Guide to Web Search Engines:
A Handbook for the Serious Searcher
By Randolph E. Hock
"Extreme searcher" Randolph (Ran) Hock—internationally respected Internet trainer and authority on Web search engines—offers straightforward advice designed to help you get immediate results. Ran not only shows you what's "under the hood" of the major search engines, but explains their relative strengths and weaknesses, reveals their many (and often overlooked) special features, and offers tips and techniques for searching the Web more efficiently and effectively than ever. Updates and links are provided at the author's Web site.

Softbound • ISBN 0-910965-26-9 • $24.95
Hardbound • ISBN 0-910965-38-2 • $34.95

Electronic Democracy:
Using the Internet to Influence American Politics
By Graeme Browning
Here is everything you need to know to become a powerful player in the political process from your desktop. Experienced Washington reporter Graeme Browning (*National Journal*, Center for Democracy & Technology) offers real-world strategies for using the World Wide Web to reach and influence decision makers inside the Beltway. Loaded with practical tips, techniques, and case studies, this is a must-read for anyone interested in the future of representative government and the marriage of technology and politics.

Softbound • ISBN 0-910965-20-X • $19.95

The Internet Unplugged:
Utilities & Techniques for Internet Productivity...Online and Off
By Michael A. Banks
Here is the first complete guide to the online and off-line "extras" every Windows user needs to make productive use of the Net. Author Michael Banks demystifies all the important software tools, shows where to find them, and offers tips and techniques for using them effectively.

Softbound • ISBN 0-910965-24-2 • $29.95

Design Wise:
A Guide for Evaluating the Interface Design of Information Resources
By Alison Head

> "*Design Wise* takes us beyond what's cool and what's hot and
> shows us what works and what doesn't."
> -Elizabeth Osder, *The New York Times on the Web*

Knowing how to size up user-centered interface design is becoming as important for people who choose and use resources as for those who design them. This book introduces readers to the basics of interface design and explains why a design evaluation should be integrally tied to what we trade cash for, trundle back in our arms, and fire up for everyone else to use—in settings of all kinds and sizes.
Softbound • ISBN 0-910965-31-5 • $29.95

Finding Images Online:
ONLINE USER's Guide to Image Searching in Cyberspace
By Paula Berinstein

While text research has been done at the desk for years, finding images has traditionally meant either relying on professional stock image houses or engaging in long, often fruitless searches. Today, cyberspace is exploding with millions of digital images, many of them in the public domain. With a personal computer, a modem, and this book, you can learn to efficiently evaluate, search, and use the vast image resources of the Internet and online services plus powerful databases designed specifically for image searchers.
Softbound • ISBN 0-910965-21-8 • $29.95

Finding Statistics Online:
How to Locate the Elusive Numbers You Need
By Paula Berinstein

Need statistics? Find them more quickly and easily than ever—online! Finding good statistics is a challenge for even the most experienced researcher. Today, it's likely that the statistics you need are available online—but where? This book explains how to effectively use the Internet and professional online systems to find the statistics you need to succeed.
Softbound • 0-910965-25-0 • $29.95

Secrets of the Super Net Searchers:
The Reflections, Revelations and Hard-Won Wisdom of 35 of the World's Top Internet Researchers
By Reva Basch

Reva Basch, whom *WIRED Magazine* has called "The Ultimate Intelligent Agent," delivers insights, anecdotes, tips, techniques, and case studies through her interviews with 35 of the world's top Internet hunters and gatherers. These Super Net Searchers explain how to find valuable information on the Internet, distinguish cyber-gems from cyber-junk, avoid "Internet Overload," and much more.
Softbound • ISBN 0-910965-22-6 • $29.95